POETRY NOW

POETRY NOW NORTH WEST 1997

Edited by Andrew Head

First published in Great Britain in 1996 by
POETRY NOW
1-2 Wainman Road, Woodston,
Peterborough, PE2 7BU

HB ISBN 1 86188 478 8
SB ISBN 1 86188 473 7

FOREWORD

Although we are a nation of poetry writers we are accused of not reading poetry and not buying poetry books: after many years of listening to the incessant gripes of poetry publishers, I can only assume that the books they publish, in general, are books that most people do not want to read.

Poetry should not be obscure, introverted, and as cryptic as a crossword puzzle: it is the poet's duty to reach out and embrace the world.

The world owes the poet nothing and we should not be expected to dig and delve into a rambling discourse searching for some inner meaning.

The reason we write poetry (and almost all of us do) is because we want to communicate: an ideal; an idea; or a specific feeling. Poetry is as essential in communication, as a letter; a radio; a telephone, and the main criteria for selecting the poems in this anthology is very simple: they communicate.

Faced with hundreds of poems and a limited amount of space, the task of choosing the final poems was difficult and as editor one tries to be as detached as possible (quite often editors can become a barrier in the writer-reader exchange) acting as go between, making the connection, not censoring because of personal taste.

'In every volume of poems something good may be found.' (Samuel Johnson)

In a world with many social and political issues we all have our own opinions. But with so many contrasting views, it is often difficult to get our voice heard.

Perhaps one of the most successful ways to communicate is through poetry, where the poets can be honest and truthful without the interference of a difference of opinion.

Poetry Now North West 1997 has brought together the voices of today's generation in a collection of poetry which communicates directly with the reader.

The poems vary in form and style; some modern, some traditional.. The themes also vary, including love, war, death, people and politics which have moved poets throughout the ages.

This anthology represents the up and coming poets of North West and the issues that inspire their poetry.

The success of this collection, and all previous *Poetry Now* anthologies, relies on the fact that there are as many individual readers as there are writers.

CONTENTS

PARTY POEM

It is Christmas time at Whiteholme? The party is in full swing?
Jim is singing 'White Christmas' and trying to sound like Bing.

Betty and Doris were dancing? Just gliding around the floor?
Cyril had drunk all the whiskey? And shouting his head off for more.

The members think this is smashing and enjoying a really good night.
The Keep-Fit were doing the Can-Can and ee by gum what a sight.

Arthur is waiting for the raffle, he is hoping to win first prize,
It might be a case of Tetley's or Cinderella in disguise.

So join in the Christmas carols and sing shout and cheer,
Wish everyone a Merry Christmas and a very prosperous New Year.

E A Daws

BORN TO QUESTION

Born to question
An unenviable plight.
Got to keep going
Such a long flight,

Finding answers one by one,
Revealing questions on and on,
The ultimate question
Will we ever reveal,

Lord why did you make us feel?
Instincts would have been enough.
But in your image we must fly,
Many tears fall from our eye,
Until we all pass by.

Rod Pilkington

SADNESS

Sadness is now
When no-one will listen
Sadness is when
Solutions never glisten
Sadness is regret
For things in the past
Sadness is lies
The truth never lasts
Sadness is silence
Or a deafening sound
Sadness is thoughts
That go round and round
Sadness is one
Here on my own
Sadness is knowledge
For all I have known
Sadness is pain
Because no-one can hear
Sadness is you
I wish you were here

Melanie Harrison

LOVE

Love is a foolish thing
You fall in it
You cry 'cause of it
You could die 'cause of it.
You think that love
Is a kiss and a cuddle.
But in your head.
It's just a muddle.

Kate Louise Harrison

JORDAN

Jordan has his toys
And his voice is clear
When he wants some more
Of those which to him are dear.
Whenever my sister's out shopping
She visits a certain store
Where giraffes, lions and monkeys
Clutter up behind the door,
Jord has great fun
As he enjoys a run
From here to there,
But alas the animals
Just seem to wear.
Children's World is the place
Where the animals are present,
Different colours
Bright and very pleasant.

Richard Long

COME VISIT THE DAWN

Arise and visit the oncoming dawn
The ray of light mending the day

Come first dull streaks into dark
Followed quickly by a frosty grey.

Then moves this gloom and opens wide
A space of the purest and brightest hues

Here cometh the sun and the clouds
Intermingled with red and blues.

Jack Taylor

A VICTIM OF WAR

I was born in a land across the sea
I'm not yet one but no-one wants me
My parents were killed not long after I was born
The country in which I live is war-torn

My mum protected me before she died
Her body for a shield did she provide
Dad protected us as best he could
But he died face down in the mud

Now I am left in this world on my own
There is nowhere I can call my home
Will anybody ever rescue me
Or is a short life my destiny?

I am only a baby what harm can I do?
Are you going to kill me too?
Is there anyone out there who will hear my plea
And let me live to be free?

Their laughter was cruel as they picked me up
They jeered 'What shall we do with this pup?'
It didn't bother them when I did cry
Just throw him to one side and let him die

As I lie here twisted and in pain
I wonder if I will see daylight again
As the numbness overtakes me and my life slips away
I wonder what is so important that my life is the pay

From my earthly home I now depart
My short life barely had a start
Is all the hatred and fighting worth it? Does it have to be?
Does killing innocent babies bring them nearer to victory?

Patricia May

PRAYER WEEK

The candles are dimmed
And all was quiet
You could feel the presence
           of our Heavenly Lord
'I gave my prayer in sweet content
Knowing it was time good spent'
You spoke to me and all was well
I thank You for that Unity
I asked for all our Brothers and
           Sisters and Fellowmen
To be heard in this Your week
Guide us to Your heavenly seat
May we know fulfilment
In communion of thought
To shine a love divine
I'm so happy Lord You made me Thine
I could not face my life without
Your help and guidance by my side
So I pray once more
That You may give
Your Loving Reverence for all who live
And show us the way
To be still and know Thou art there.

Mabel

REFLECTED GLORY

You all write your verse of Tom Finney the great
Outside right for England, but what of his mate?
The one who's behind him, the one who's in charge
Of his health and his welfare, no I don't mean George Bargh

I mean Elsie his wife, whom you don't often see
In the limelight with Tom but I think you'll agree
That without her help he'd be in a flat spin
And could not play well, or help North End to win

She cooks and she mends for 'Our Tom' as I know
And cleans and looks after their cute bungalow
So as you watch Tom on the field as he plays
Give a thought to his wife, who spends all of her days
Keeping happy Tom Finney and his family
A boy and girl who are pretty to see

Three cheers for Elsie who keeps Tom 'up to scratch'
And so gets him known as 'The Man of the Match'.

Tess Whitlock

THE YORKSHIRE MOORS

And all about me moor and sky
Upon my senses now impinge,
A sense of freedom, swept with joy
That lifts my soul on feathered wings

My eyes drink in the timeless scene,
As sunlight moves upon its face
And clouds build castles, tall, pristine,
On blue infinite space

The rolling moors whose grasses grow
With colours ever changing
Majestic 'neath the winds that blow,
Their wildness not for taming

How often, with an inward glance,
I gaze upon this scene,
And in that moment am at once
Upon the moors, with wind, unseen.

J Mackereth

GOD'S PHILHARMONIC

As I sat by the shore - sweet music I heard.
The purest melody - like the song of a bird.
A *crash* on a cymbal - a sigh of the strings.
A brush on a snare drum - like soft beating wings.
Up to a crescendo - then back down again . . .
like the sun's blazing glory - to soft falling rain.
Whence came this music? This God's symphony!
It came from the tide's edge - and the great open sea.
White horses came racing - their hooves gave the beat;
quiet wavelets withdrawing - the melody to complete.
Small pebbles and sand - falling back with them
all had combined - to give it its rhythm.
Then various sea shells - broken and sharp
rolling and tinkling - like a trill on a harp.
Then loudly and strong - like a military band
the waves came a-crashing - again on the sand!
As I left, shingle rolling - as if saluting a cause,
gave the standing ovation - supplied the applause!

H Ashbee-Robinson

WINTER DRIVE

Hanni, I remember what you say about the quality of light,
as I speed along from Sedburgh to Haws.

I remember your delight, as evening falls and orange light
softens the jagged stonewalls,
that stitch the fell sides.

But this is deep winter
and the cold is raw,
one of those that happens every ten years
and you know that all these walls and gnarly oaks have seen
at least a dozen as cold as this.

I'm warm in the van, as the engine blurts its message
through the broken exhaust.
I gun the engine to emphasise its tone.

Drifts drift by, sullied snow swept into deep steep grubby folds
alongside the road
On a sharp bend a farmhouse roof dotted with cats' paw prints
to a window winking warmth.

Figures on the white slopes spreadeagle themselves
on plastic toboggans and skydive headfirst down the slope.

Screaming as they deathslide back into childhood,
escaping the humdrum
revelling in the finger numbing free play of winter.

J C France

THE SONG

See the little bird up in the tree. She is singing her heart out
          for you and me.
See the branches swaying to and fro in the breeze,
As the wind carries her song far away until it reaches the sea
The waves then clasp the song and leave it upon the shores
          of a far distant land
See the dolphins swim about in the sea.
They are dancing to the tune that the little bird sang.
They too will carry the song on their backs, to the very same land.
On the shores of this land, sits a lonely man.
He hears that tune, that the little bird sang
With joy in his heart, he dances his way to the village,
          to share with others, that very song.
That very song, that once was sung by a little bird up in a tree
is carried on the wind again back across the waters.
And back to you and me.

Susan Foster

ESCAPOLOGY

Writing for my freedom
Writing for a laugh,
A tome of perfect prose
Or a sonnet in the bath.

Writing always writing
Nothing really beats it,
Nothing trends can't transcend
And nothing can defeat it.

A rising independence
The words releasing me,
Chapter verse vanish curse
The sentence sets me free.

Les Lambert

9

HIDDEN TIME

Marching forward, ever on,
The pounding feet
The beat of the drum.
Khaki figures stand in line
Interspersed with blue and red, the colour of wine.

The bugles call, the men respond,
Denied their comforts,
England must stand strong.
Youthful innocents stand and fight
Torn from their loved ones, earthly delight.

Forward, ever onwards, into the void,
War leaves nothing untouched.
No innocence survives,
Bent on destruction, for their evil ends,
Parts families, loved ones and faithful friends.

Though years do pass,
Wounds of the body do heal,
But the styles of humanity, remain for all, but a few,
Those whose lives are too short, to rue.
Their echoing tramp, remains for all time.

Names long forgotten, still reveal the pain
Mons, Somme, Verdun, Ypres.
The chilling sounds of battle, echo in the trees.
Forward, ever onwards, silent they pass
Those ghostly marching soldier boys, drift past.

Jane Dyson

JIMMY

Can in hand and gap in tooth,
He drowns his sorrows in vermouth.
Or meths or something equally sad,
What murky deed sends a man this mad?

Round and round and back again,
He swigs again every now and then.
An endless hoe-down every day,
How does a man end up this way?

He reels and tumbles to the ground,
Laughs 'til he cries a babbling sound.
What once was speech is now a gibber,
What does he hide not being sober?

Shoes and socks off, on again,
But seldom does he hold a grain;
Of memory why disrobed he lay.
Why does a man end up this way?

Long ago when he could talk,
And in a straight line he could walk.
He must have mentioned what he'd done,
And why he awaits death's sweet stun gun.

Mark John Hurst

LIFE

Don't rush your life,
Don't have regrets,
Enjoy yourself,
Take every opportunity for happiness,
Don't plan too far ahead,
Just enjoy every day to the best of your ability,
Take your time,
There is no hurry to get to your destiny,
Getting there,
Is the challenge and mystery of life,
Take life's knocks and enjoy the good times,
Don't ask for too much,
And you can't be disappointed,
Do not rely on others for your happiness,
Find your own happiness in everyday life,
Be grateful for what you have
And how far you have come.

Alex Swarbrick

ECSTASY

Is it worth the pain
That comes within the joy?
Your life comes down like rain
Lives that you destroy
Leaving families broken-hearted
Bad memories remain
Your life that has departed
Has made them go insane
Because of a pill you've taken
You are history
People are mistaken
Of the pain in Ecstasy.

Emma Hughes (13)

12

MY SON

(Dedicated to my son Paul Anthony, born stillborn 16.9.63. I didn't, at the time, have the courage to look at him. But over the years I have suffered deep sorrow over the 'emotional' mistake.)

He has been gone a long time now
How I've survived I don't know how.
My love for him is still so strong;
And yet, in my heart, I know it's wrong
To keep the memories of bygone days
A part of my life in so many ways.
To mention his name is always a joy;
Reminding all of my baby boy
His time so short inside of me,
The gift of life was not to be.
A stillness at his precious birth
Denied him presence upon this earth.
A little form, disfigured, yet new
Faded away like the morning dew.

My emptiness, and grief, at not seeing him
Has been my torment for this terrible sin.
If only I had touched his tiny cheek
To vent the emotions I could not speak
'I love you my child, little fragile one.'
But life for him had not begun.
He was taken away before I could see
His lifeless body looking at me.
Please God, I pray, in time to come
You will unite me with my darling son.

Jean Davies

13

STREETS OF LIVERPOOL

When it rains, it rains circles
In the pools on the shore
And there'll always be a rainbow
And there will be evermore
When the sun, rising high
Comes to take its daily rule
I'll sit and I'll dream
Of the streets of Liverpool

When you gaze across the river
You'll conjure a bonny sight
Of fair ould Emerald Ireland
Be it sunny day or night
And further on an ocean
Makes our river look a pool
Here I'll sit and dream
Of the streets of Liverpool

Above the sparkling sapphire waves
Which loll onto the beach
As gentle as a lullaby
As soft as whispered speech
Below an orange ring of heat
In azure sky so cool
I'll sit and I'll dream
Of the streets of Liverpool

Never will I listen to
Or hear the dreamless fool
Who tells me that my image
Is not the streets of Liverpool.

Kerry Hughes (14)

GRANDAD

Grandad's gone to heaven
That's what my daddy said
I saw my auntie crying
When she was putting me to bed

My grandad was an old man
With a twinkle in his eye
He told me lots of stories
Why did he have to die?

I've lost someone who taught me
What it was to have a friend
I helped him in his greenhouse
I gave him toys to mend

He helped me with my paintings
I helped him sowing seeds
We'd potter in the garden
And pull up all the weeds

Soon I will be older
And then I'll understand
Why grandads go to heaven
And we are left behind

Now all I have are memories
And Grandad's up above
But memories I'll cherish
Of a grandad truly loved

A Noonan

STUCK!

I worked in a garden, made things grow,
I'd a spade, fork, trowel and a hoe,
In those days, I just didn't realise,
Compared to now, I was working in Paradise,
A good job, but the wage was poor,
We'd started a family and needed more,
I thought 'I can get no more here,'
So I started to look for a new career,
To the factory I made my way,
After a while, I'd doubled my old pay,
Working funny hours, and the job is harder,
But the bills are paid, and we've a full larder,
There's chemicals and a funny smell,
Sometimes I think 'This place is hell!'
Today it seems that we are wealthy,
Tomorrow, however, I might not be healthy,
I'd like to get out and go elsewhere,
But the money's good and I don't dare,
Just lately the shifts, have made me tired and sad,
I've shouted at my family, that's made me feel bad,
Hoping and dreaming of things to do and be,
Millions, think the same as me,
Pick yourself up man, you have to carry on,
If that ship comes in, though, we're gone!

Christopher D Sykes

GOOD MORNING WORLD

The morning mist rises
carefully revealing the land to the world
varying shades of green and yellow
fields rolling away to the horizon
mountains standing majestically
like great Gods, surveying all below
birds take to the wing in the first light
breaking the silence with their chorus
other signs of life appear
the world begins to wake
the sun emerges
smearing gold everywhere
pushing night to whence it came
taking over the world
with a clear blue sky
Good morning dawning

E M Gillespie

HOME-SHY

cavilling sages
cardboard cages
bodies a-trembling
closely assembling

careful charm
lingering harm
absent protection
pointless injection

outwardly reeling
inwardly feeling
. hole bolt
arch vault

David Torrens

60'S CONSTRUCTION WORKER

Railway station, suitcase, hard hats, toe tectors, Simon and Garfunkel,
Homeward Bound.
Another Monday, another town, sleet lashing their faces
from dark ominous skies.
They troop pilgrim-like to waiting coaches, close ranks on foreign ground.
Strange looking pilgrims these, thick set, broad shouldered,
faces weathered, heads held high.

They're drawn, as if by unseen forces, to new sites and freshly erected
steelwork
Working long, dangerous shifts on rigs and chemical plant, paid
in money and pain.
Industrial nomads, sparks riggers, fitters, welders, always chasing the perks
Hours booked on, a Friday flyer, extras needed for life in the fast lane.

They clocked on next day heads sore from the bevvy, the conditions
not fit for a dog.
There's ice on the steel, snow falling thick and the chargehand's
growling for blood.
'We must progress the job, there's work undercover, and I'll sack
any men in the bog.'
A sudden roar of laughter, the Agent's slipped, broke his arm,
he's outside on his arse, in the mud.

They're sat in a cabin, beige coloured, eighty yards long, it's used
as the site canteen.
Eggs, bacon, sausage, chips and beans, tea, bread and butter
are served up all day.
Also accommodated are card schools, some quiet, some wild, all deadly
keen.
High stake games, violent deaths, vicious beatings, the turn of a card
on a fortnight's pay.

Three thousand workers down tools, hold a mass meeting outside the gates.
A total stoppage, no surrender, the Steward's conned
into another no-win fight.
'We need them out for a month. No discussions on conditions, hours or rates.'

18

Management's delighted, the blueprints are wrong, there's no work
until they're put right.

How many survive when that final shift's done, as age and illness
take their toll?
Just their memories left of twenty years chasing that
illusive crock of gold.
Disillusioned, bodies knackered, lungs wrecked, unable to fulfil life's goals.
The good times long gone, they remember the crack, remember
their mates on the road.

T R Bates

BOSNIA

They came upon the ancient city
gripping their modern weapons
and laid waste my home
in but a matter of seconds

Rubble and remnants now
the only trace a dimming twilight
in the minds of the old and the weak

A familiar taste
the rambling ruins of a disused farmhouse
where friends and I would play

No more now
not tomorrow or the next
children no more

To martyrs and the elderly
war strikes a bitter blow
but the full depth of its shadow
only the children come to know.

John Derek Flanagan

WHICH WAY TO GO

Don't be filled with regret,
For ambitions never met,
Or young love forever smitten,
A love letter never given.
Everything happens for a reason.
After spring comes another season.
Winter's gone and things grow fresh again,
Everything's brighter after the rain.
And clearer after the snow,
Somehow we know which way to go.

Angela Johnson

MY GARDEN

Oh I have a wonderful garden - perhaps not so special to you
But mine is a garden of memories of friends so kind-hearted and true.
It consists of a real good assortment of blooms as the seasons go by
And each day I visit its corner to see how its progress may lie.
The first shoots of snowdrops appearing, the crocus and daffies come next
And the joy which it always affords me is soothing when I am perplexed.
As the seasons go by an appearance of species once more I can see,
And I think of the joys and the sorrows when friends brought
their brightness to me.
There's a rosebush when given one birthday, a lilac tree when sorrow maimed
Chrysanthemums given to cheer me when sickness my body sustained
Anemones bold from some children, a fern tree to brighten my day
A ladslove from one of my colleagues and sweet peas with colour so gay
So many bright hues now confront me as the garden I often survey -
My garden of friendship - what more could one ask?
Bringing memories of love all the way.

Gladys Roberts

UNTITLED

I cannot make the sun to shine,
Or hang the amber moon,
I cannot usher in the dawn,
Or warm the day at noon,
I cannot light a firefly,
Or catch an early dew,
I cannot build a mountain,
With peaks of purple hue;
I cannot make the winds to blow,
Or stop the rain on you,
I cannot make the rivers flow,
Or make the skies ablue,
I cannot make the flowers blossom
Or make the starving few,
I cannot give the world more peace,
Or make old things anew,
Our world is full of many things,
That I could never do,
But I can build a bridge of love,
To reach from me to you.

Gary Baxter

LIVE AND LET LIVE

Live and let live
The way our world should be
Freedom for you
Freedom for me
Freedom for all
Be you black
Be you white
Freedom for all
It's only right

Alan Green

THE OWL

Owl of the wildwood I;
Muffled in sleep I drowse,
Where no fierce sun in heaven
Can me arouse.

My haunt's a hollow
In a half-dead tree,
Whose strangling ivy
Shields and shelters me.

But when dark's starlight
Thrids my green domain,
My plumage trembles and stirs,
I awake again;

A spectral moon
Silvers the world I see;
Out of their day-long lairs
Creep thievishly

Night living things.
Then I,
Wafted away on soundless pinions
Fly;
Curdling her arches
With my hunting cry;
A-hooh! A-hooh!

Four notes, and then,
Solemn, sepulchral, cold,
Four notes again,
The listening dingles
Of my woodland through;
A-hooh! A-hooh! -
A-hooh!

Patricia McKeenan

LOST LOVE

I can get through the whole day now without thinking of you,
Without seeing your face,
Hearing your voice,
I am stronger now.

My heart aches with a heaviness that consumes me.
The nights are long and lonely.
I long to touch you,
Feel you near me.

When I am alone I escape into a state of ecstasy,
Would that I could stay in this repose.
When you are with me I am fulfilled.

Help me! I am searching but finding nothing,
Looking but seeing nothing,
Feeling but touching nothing,
Set me free, take my hand lead me.

There is a world out there,
I have to join it.
Take my hurt away,
Make me see I am alive,
I will live.

Love cannot destroy me.

Joyce Hampson

MANY KINDS OF LOVE

Oh Love, if that is your name
You take my heart, crush it, bringing me pain
I thought to love, would bring peace to my heart
To be near them, close to them, never to part,
Oh Love, you have more than one face
Which one do I embrace?

The love I have for my parents
They are gone now, but the love is still there
My sisters and brothers still get their share
The love I have for my husband
Growing stronger, day by day.
The love I have for my children
Never never to go away.

The little ones, oh so much love I have for them
Yet where does all this love come from?
Again, and again, yet again
Suddenly I knew the answer
I should have known it from the start.
It was God, who put so much love in my heart.

Irene McSorley

CHRISTMAS TIME

Cold winds with snow, outside the house
Through frost and ice, there's ne'er a mouse
But children on the pond all skate
With Mums and Dads, who shout and wait.

Until upon the ground made white
Descends the dark, and with it night.
Church bells sounding loud and clear,
Their Christmas call, for you to hear.

Much laughter, in the cold still night.
Their bobbing lamps, all shining bright
In voices old, and voices young,
Those age-old tunes, of carols sung.

Till rising sun, on frosty hill
Pass silent snowmen, glistening, still
On church's spire, and weather vane
I know each year will be the same.

I see it all, through window pane.

J M H Barton

CHEMICAL BRAINS

Chemical brains sit alone in the room
frightened of leaving their guilt-ridden tomb.
There's a smile on their lips but it's just a disguise,
for they can't hide the pain that burns in their eyes.
It's a pain they're aware of but one they don't need,
that festers inside like an alien breed.
'Won't somebody help me?' their eyes seem to shout,
but their plea stays unanswered, there's no-one about.
It's just them and their world they've created inside,
with nowhere to run so there's nowhere to hide.
Just lost in a chasm of nightmares and pain,
endlessly floating through oceans of rain,
these paranoid minds play their own cruel games,
like pointing the finger and calling out names.
Their twisted assortment of personal grief
helps no-one least them to dispatch their relief.
The solution's quite simple, it's easy to fix.
A brain and a chemical really don't mix.

Brian Jolley

FRUSTRATED SILENCE

Born without sound, heard no mother's lullaby,
No loudness of laugh, never heard myself cry.

Standing alone in silence, that only I know,
I'm a world apart, which to you doesn't show.
My eyes are good, my brain intact,
But I'm not one of you, and that is a fact.

It was hard at school, you must speak with a voice,
I'd rather have signed, but was offered no choice.
The hearing know best, and paternalism rules,
Deaf and dumb is the label, but we deaf are not fools.

Why pass me by, with just a nod and a smile?
Try to communicate, you could learn in a while.
Don't stare when I sign, I have words of my own,
Fingers that talk, and in books they are shown.

I look at you, and my heart screams out,
I would love to whisper, I would love to shout.
How do I find a good job, I feel so left out.

Learn about me, I have so much to give,
And allow me to join in, where the hearing world live.

I know you may think, that I keep to my own,
But it's impossible to escape, from this silence I've known.
Just offer your hand, and my language I'll lend,
Then my deafness will be, no barrier to a friend.

Brian John Nicholson

UNTITLED

A smile so sweet
A kiss so tender
The thread of love - so strong
Yet slender
A heart so full
A life to live
Everything to hope for
Everything to give
Nothing lasts forever
Life is so unkind
Bring it all back
Let the clocks all rewind
Take me back to happy times
When everything seemed clear
Take me back to anywhere
Just take me out of here.

Anita J Jones

INSPIRATIONS FROM GRASMERE

God's creation all around us,
Running streams and rivers flow,
Awesome beauty, lakes and forests
Summer sunshine casts a glow.

Mountains rise in all their glory,
Everywhere is so serene,
Radiant fields where sheep are grazing,
Every wood is fresh and green.

Let me stand and pause a moment,
At the wonders of the land,
Thank our Father for these treasures,
Made by His Almighty Hand.

Kathleen Barras

ODE TO A DEEP FREEZER

I've never been a star on any level of domesticity
And no-one is more thankful for gadgets run by electricity
I'm not cleaning to eat off the floor of my bungalow
And I don't need my kitchen to sparkle and glow

The advent of frozen food I would never disparage
How did we manage without a freezer in the garage?
There must be other freezers harbouring secrets at the bottom
And any food from A to Z, if you want 'em - I got 'em.

Two lamb chops past sell-by date by about three years
A bag containing a chicken of the sort Edwina Curry fears
There must be salmonella and germs breeding like rabbits
A few shrimps and a couple of old trout with very peculiar habits

There are Weight Watcher's packs from when I was slimming
Non-glutinous foods from when my blood needed thinning
Frozen orange juice from when that's all I could sup
And fresh cream doughnuts from when I gave all that up.

There are four mince tarts left from the Christmas before last
Half a bag of sprouts that wouldn't survive a micro-wave blast
There's fish fingers, vegetable lasagne and half a turkey breast
If you'd like to unravel more secrets, please, come on, be my guest.

Florence Broomfield

DRESSING FOR THE OCCASION

No chequebook needed, credit card,
no cash in pocket.
To stay in fashion not too hard
- nor something to regret
for one whose entire patterning
undergoes swift changes . . .

damson. Deep blue. Or - green-swaying
where, sharp-eyed, it ranges,
at one with its environment.
Like seaweed. Or like sand.
Now seeking prey for its nourishment . . .
unbelievably bland . . .

Once aware of another's greed
it turns into coral -
to which a large fish pays no heed
fooled by its apparel.

Yes. Watch this fish wear stripe on stripe
or, suddenly, show spots
apple-green, cherry ripe,
a shining silver with black dots . . .

Now garish. Now less obvious . . .
Sinuous. Elegant . . .
Yet no change simply capricious
. . . too insignificant

to be overlooked -

Strategy
- combined with artistry -

A chameleon must envy
such changes in the sea.

C M Creedon

UTOPIA

Here we stand in line,
At our allotted times and spaces,
And sign pieces of paper,
With expressionless faces,
Just another number,
On their computer.

I remember employment,
In the days when life was sweet,
But now I walk down,
The rain sodden street,
The factories are closing,
Some have gone for good,
Where generations worked,
There remains only rubble and mud.

Developers are busy building,
Houses for the privileged few,
There is no place in their dreams,
For people like me and you,
The lucky ones at least,
Have roofs over their heads,
While others have cardboard boxes,
For their beds.

Those in high places, spend millions,
On wild schemes and war,
And yet they cannot give us jobs,
Or even a penny more,
Politicians promise us the earth,
But only when they are elected,
Do we see what their words are worth.

Karl Becker

A CHILD CAN BE . . .

Me on my own,
Me all alone,
Me with a child of three.

A baby just newly born can be
Well they have a tendance to cry,
But only for their dinner,
Lunch and tea.
But also bring you happiness,
Every single day.

A child of one can be,
Shall we say distressing?
But also cute and caring too.

A child of three can be,
Well, I would say
Just a little picky.
But always happy
And willing to share.

A child of four can be,
Well, I'm not sure,
But I'm sure,
She'll be telling me
Exactly when it's time
For tea.
But I'll love her
All the same.

L A Smith

THE CONSEQUENCES OF THE HOUND'S SCENT

The consequences of the hound's scent;
Flimsy fox;
Floating.

Blood-raw paw stroking the reeves of the sodden bank,
Positioning itself as to raise,
Its body.

Slumped lifeless remains;
Conscience caressing
Despair.

Head to the side
Ear to the ground, cocked,
Tenderly aware of endless sounds beneath.

Eye clenches again, feel of
Pain again.
Glimpses to view red gashes, scratches.
Eye clenches again.

Toyed with being.
Drooping eyes break day.
Endless sleep to lands above the rickety plain.
Dies.

Skies give way, open, release unwittingly,
Rain plummets, slumps off lifeless body.
Snow falls.

Jonathan Child

FEAR

(A cable-car ride across the straits from Singapore to Sentosa Island)

Brightly coloured cable-car approaches swinging;
We climb aboard in cheerful haste.
Away we go - the view is stunning,
Skyscrapers dwarfed along the coast.
I look behind;
The cable is sagging,
And far below
Ocean vessels churn.
I freeze, immobilised in my swaying prison.
The midway tower hauls us higher again.
Gritted teeth clench a scream.
Down again - the island draws nearer,
With tall trees like velvet to cushion a fall.
Sentosa the fortress, the playground, museum,
How welcome your flowers, your beaches, lagoon!
But oh! How the thought chills
Of early returning!
Admit to my terror?
Hope for a high wind
To close down the ride?
But no - three hours later
The bright coloured carriage swings closer again,
But this time I *don't* look,
I focus my camera, adjusting its view with meticulous aim.
The ride seems much shorter,
The wire troughs much gentler,
In no time it seems we're safe landed again.

L J Spencer

BLIND FAITH

'Jump!' bids the preacher,
And the believer, diseased with sin,
Flings his rotting soul down,
Down into the mouth of moral sanctuary.

'Jump!' smirks the leader.
And the people consenting to his lies as truth,
Raise their hands in salute to their coloured material,
And title their eyeless obedience, patriotism.

'Jump!' calls the father.
And for his heritage, soldier-hero pulls out his gun.
In some foreign land, laughing faces crumple
To cold surprise, and blood suffocates the twilight.

'Jump!' cries the mother.
And her shame-bringing, name-dragging daughter,
Presses the other heart beating within her stomach,
Before she lets it be took, half-formed from her.

'Jump!' whispers the lover,
And the Juliet pauses before the moon,
Because of forbidden love, cuts,
The weak threads of her throbbing pulse.

'Jump!' the voice tells each man.
'Jump. Down below, into my arms. I will catch you!'
When man peers over the precipice
And sees nothing but blackness,
He turns around and asks the unaskable question: 'Why?'
The silence of no-reply hangs in the still air.
Instead from the shadows,
A hand reaches out,
And pushes him off the cliff edge
For daring to ask the unaskable question.

Farah Shaheen

UNTITLED

I kiss your lips,
Then taste their sweetness,
Just as surely as the new day,
Greets the dawn.

Then as I face that day,
You fill my heart,
And mind,
With sounds of love.

The thoughts of you,
Held gently,
In my arms,
A loving word,
A touch.

And then,
I die,
Until I'm with you,
Once again.

To taste once more,
Your honeyed kiss,
To help me,
Through another day.

Frank Watson

LIVING A LIFE

When day is done
And my body exhausted,
I do lay down
Upon life's precious thing

Maybe for an hour
Maybe for the day
Who knows, maybe forever
My weary bones will rest

My dreams are never far away
And nor is my reality
For the things to reach
Which we think is unreachable,

My goals set high
A task I set myself,
My whole life do I have
To accomplish my ambition

If I work from morn to dusk
And study in between,
The higher the task I set
The easier it will be to reach

I won't give up hope
Because it starts to get hard,
For the harder it gets
The more knowledge do I absorb

For I do have faith
In what I believe in,
Rather than what I don't
Which makes life that much easier.

S J Davidson

SHOPPING ODE TO SANDY BROOK

Sandy Brook still sounds the same
Refreshing, clean, alive
If I did not bother to take a look
I would not know it had died.
The clear water right for a paddling place
Swimming with assorted fish
A bank of silver sand to sit and play and wish
To lie under the blossom tree painting pictures of the clouds in the sky
Not caring about time, hours drifting by
But now your infected flush seems uncertain where to go
Fast and lively yesterday now 'tallow' is your flow
Rubbish swims instead of fish
Your banks crawl with weeds
Country paths overgrown beneath the dying trees
I pity what my children miss
The beauty that shone from your face
To them Sandy Brook is just another dirty place.

L Petherwick

I'M SORRY

I hit with the hand
That was to caress,
And cursed with the mouth
That meant just to kiss,
And I could say sorry
A thousand more times
But you asked me to go
And you've made up your mind.
You've nothing to lose
Yet you've nothing to gain,
And nursing the bruise
Only adds to the pain.

Natalia Perry

A SON'S HAND

Such a tiny hand.
Five perfect little fingers
Exploring your new world
Stretching and curling
Encircling my finger and my heart.

Such a dirty hand.
What have you been doing?
Finger painting, mud pies
Playground grazes
Kindergarten size.

Such a clever hand.
You made your first catch today -
A new Ian Botham on the pitch,
The next Will Carling so they say
He's got good hands.

Such gentle hands
Stroking your first puppy
Cupping a young girl's face
Tracing her body lightly
Grown up hands.

Such a big hand
It holds both mine now.
Am I ready to let go
As you explore the wider world
And wave goodbye?

Jeffa Kay

ETHEREAL HAIKU

Scent of rain on grass
driving me crazy with life
grasp it quickly now

loving spiny fish
look at you with glass-bowl eyes
glancing kiss your skin

laughing in the rain
the morning after kissing
sandals in my hand

blossom kiss on wind
floats through my open window
wedding thoughts fall down

dancing tree shadows
evening closes gently round
stars the only sound

Sarah Humphreys

GOODNIGHT

Keep away your sullen skies.
Lightning flash as thunder roars.
Artillery cries, commotion.
Violent rumbles from another world.
Rain swept hills.
A gushing sigh.
Pray God for us a silent night.

Jon Aspinall

THE WHISPER OF LIFE

Step out of the darkness
Into the light
And walk through the blindness into the sight
Follow the instinct
For spirits must hide
Within this secret world where time must reside

You step from a whisper
And the sentence of life
To transcend into mirage and beliefs you have stored
Your memories a library when your spirit is moored
While the trauma of living and death can be cured

Every wound you have bled
Soon shall be healed
Every moment of sorrow and trespass shall yield
The prejudice that haunts you
Now asks for release
For you're shouldered with the judgement only your conscience can lease

Every burden you placed
Became strewn in your path
For the learning of spirit within body is yours
You were the teacher and the pupil you taught
To settle like sand on the edge of these shores

This is the tomorrow
The Avalon of belief
The womb of forever on this loved hallowed turf
But sometimes a murmur
And a thought can be heard
'Tis the whisper of life from the twilight of Earth

David Bridgewater

THE VISITORS

What a beautiful afternoon.
The May sun teasing
With summer-like days.
All the guests arriving
In all their different ways.
It was strange to see
Such a gathering,
Especially
In my own front room.
To see for me so many,
Yet for years
I haven't seen any.
I feel warm with
The company,
And everyone
So nice,
And pleased to see me.
I would love to stay here
Forever,
But I would be late
For my own funeral!

Chris Alexander

SACK

You know you
        have
           been
a development.

So long now these words have been
used to enable all and sundry
from being able to carry 56 lbs of spuds.

Steve Town

BEYOND THE WINDOW

Alive is out, there
Just beyond the glass partition
Alive is sights and smells and air
Opposed to stale and empty wishing
Alive is roads that end tomorrow
And tomorrow is always another day
Here is constantly today, a mere existence
Alive is mapping out the future
Here is acting out this play
Out there is anger, out there is pain
Out there is love, joy, sunshine, rain
In here is hours lost
Minutes saved, seconds ticking by
A wasted stagnant
Mountain of time

Steffi Jay

NOTHING OF CONSEQUENCE

What are you doing this afternoon?
Nothing of consequence.
Nothing worth singling out as an event.
My time is often squandered,
not spent,
changing my life
or yours,
or ours,
with constructively choreographed hours,
shooting my arrows
at targets unseen.
My afternoons are more often used
to keep our clothes and humble home
clean.

John Tirebuck

42

REDUNDANT STATION

Once this place had a name,
Plainly painted on a board -
This place is 'Somewhere'.

Trains stopped at this station,
People came and went,
There was bustle and clamour,
Trundling of trolleys, mail bags
Stacked in the van or thrown
Carelessly out of doors.
The station master condescendingly
Paced out the platform's length
Eyeing the busyness, before
The guard green-flagged and whistled
And the train departed.

Now, disrespectful weeds
Thrust through the tarmac,
Where long-discarded sleepers lie
With rusted rails, where yesterday
Feet hurried to and fro.
Buildings subside in sad decay.
The moaning wind
Conjures up ghostly voices.
The Inter-City thunders through
Weed-wasted 'Somewhere',
Which slowly, yet inexorably,
Sinks into oblivion.

Margaret Lenn

SILENCE IS AN EMPTY HEART

Silence is an empty heart
When love has become sour
Silence is a lonely heart
Each minute seems an hour

Silence is oppressive
When a marriage has been sundered
Silence is the sound we hear
When love of life is plundered

Silence is the healing balm
We need in time of sorrows
Silence is the sound we hear
When there'll be no more tomorrows

Silence is an empty shore
With waves so gently lapping
Silence is the end of time
The sound of one hand clapping

Silence is a velvet fog
That covers thick and deep
Silence can be golden
It also can be cheap

Silence is a broken word
A promise not fulfilled
Silence is when hope is gone
And all emotion stilled

B B Hurst

STROKE

A blind
bars the window.
I wait for visiting time.

A shadow cuts the room
in two.
Half of me is eclipsed by a moon.

I search under a sheet
of darkness
and find a stranger asleep.

We might as well be
in separate beds.
You will not respond to me.

The words will not come
when I want,
they work my lips and tongue.

A physiotherapist
bends limbs,
like lead pipe, at knee and wrist,

jerks me from the bed,
tickles my foot.
Toes turn up. Am I dead?

Half of me says no,
grasps my sleeping hand,
will not let go.

Chris Woods

INNOCENCE LIKE A DOVE

For if this pastel shade of an evening were human,
it would be kissed by those with a pastel shaded heart
and held tight in an affectionate grip.

That's a daylight thought while travelling along a
road on Lancashire with people that you can call friends,
because you know some of us have been prisoned in a cell
of selfishness in an immoral world, like a dirty street
with bad sanitation leaking from beneath and travelling
down the gutter.

And don't we feel sad for some, where innocence like a dove
in slow motion left a heart full of love and kindness,
could be a street walker, an empty talker, a thief, a beggar,
even the rich man.

Innocence like a dove, underneath, some of us, we are.

Alison McGinty

TABOO

Some situations should never arise:
They tell us that in our lives
We should stay with our own
Class, religion, race, generation:
Society's plan - unwritten, but known.

Men are mere machines,
There to plant basic seeds,
Then leave their part through,
And women should be of age to reproduce,
Or why bother to seduce?

And never cross the class barrier -
Suburban socialists from academia
Can sympathise, patronise,
But they've never shared our lives:
It's tough being on the sides.

Never fall for an educated divorcee
In a position of authority,
Or if you find that you do,
Don't let her be older than you -
Don't break the taboo.

Peter Burns

FLIGHT

At several hundred miles an hour
The landscape slides idly by.
Sprawling settlements cluster
Like moss between flattened hills.
Cumuli cast small shadows
The size of countries.
Countries' borders are irrelevant:
The railways divide this land.
Across the densely populated swathe of Europe
No life can be seen.
All is still and quiet
From this perspective in the sky.
And the trees stand out strongly
Against Man's structured minutiae.

Then, as we travel eastwards,
A thick veil is drawn over the earth
Preventing my view.

Helen Ireson

CERTIFIED

Each man kills the thing he loves
And each girl kills her hero
A never ending spiral

Each day a little step towards doom
Knife drawer shaking dreaming a gleam
A never ending spiral

Each life comes to an end
Mine and yours his and hers
A never ending spiral

So tell me where are you now
What do you dream of think of talk of
A never ending spiral

The door is always ajar
Each girl kills the one she loves
A never ending spiral

What is love what is love
The end of a life the end of a dream
A never ending spiral

Louise Cole

LASCAUX

I went on a journey beneath the ground
In a cave of wondrous sights,
Where ancient man lived out his life
In the gloom of perpetual nights.

Deeper and deeper a way was found
Till I came to a cavernous hall,
Where mysterious symbols of birds and
Beasts were painted on every wall.

I lost myself of present time
And entered a world long ago
I imagined myself as living there
In that darkness so far below.

My journey through time left me shivering -
- And cold, I was glad to come out in the sun,
And warm myself in its glowing rays,
My journey through darkness was done.

Valerie Hall

SANTA'S VISIT

The snow is falling, the trees are white
The bells are ringing, Santa's in sight

There's presents aplenty for girls and boys
It's an exciting time to receive new toys
Put out the carrot and a glass of wine
Our Christmas stockings are stretched in a line

My eyes are heavy, I can't keep awake
Mum is icing the Christmas cake
I hear footsteps coming by the door
It's Santa, it's Santa with gifts galore

My eyes are closed, I'm falling asleep
I'm dreaming of toys piled up in a heap
In just six hours I'll jump out of bed
A visit will have been made by the man in red

The snow is falling, the trees are white
The bells are ringing, Santa's out of sight

B Porter

BANG YOU'RE DEAD
(For all IRA bombing victims)

Why is it you can't walk down the street any more,
Without a bomb going off, knocking you to the floor,
Leaving you for dead or screaming with pain?
Yes, innocent people killed by the mentally insane.
These are the acts of groups like the IRA,
Who do this sort of thing on any day,
In crowded shopping areas or just in a bin,
They keep letting the bombs off, but nobody will win.
It leaves parents and families left in tatters,
While the world grieves and helps when it matters,
What a way to put a point across,
With so much damage and human loss.
It's bad enough with war and nuclear pollution,
But we have to put up with it until there's a solution,
So will their cowardly destruction of innocence ever end
So our hearts and minds can be left to mend?
Please leave us in peace and have no more bloodshed
So then I won't have to write poems like
Bang you're dead.

D Tansley

TWINKLETOES

As I look back on my week of hell
when my baby girl she wasn't so well.
They said she's fine, there's nothing wrong,
and she'll be well before too long.

But I look at her and her glassy stare,
her usual spark it just isn't there.
The days go by and she gets worse.
To intensive care my girl is moved.

Four long days and endless nights
we're always there right by her side.
As we sit here, God hear our prayer
we just hold hands with a tearful stare.

Now my girl is fit and well,
I can now look back on my week of hell.
Now time has passed I can thank my friends
For my Twinkletoes how I would miss you.

Terence I Rush-Morgan

EXPERIENCE

Through a drunken mouth and a drunken eye; turned eastward,
upward, to a drunken sky . . . saw five famished portions
of five inner worlds - each one of them in the orbit of faces
manifest to the mind.
This experience did show the dreamer several graphic details
of a spiral in awe. All the trash of an inebriated angel
was part and parcel of a staggering whim.
Would it beg the question of this loon that the offering, in solitude,
is barmy to the moon?
Tied to his bed with the night before poison
nothing could be certain! The eyes waking with a windowlike
effect - madness is the fact catching a full vision
of the dark view.
Over my naked flesh are risen black-blue-red, with a purpleish
hue, the bruising and bitten marks of phantastic residue.
With their latest fantastic tricks the ghosts had tried to
resist the wabblings of this thick-skinned, drunken lout . . .
And failure is self-evident with the penning of such an account.

Jonathan Sutcliffe

51

INSIDE YOUR EYES

Staring into space
Seeing nothing
But your face
No emotion
No surprise
Lying there
Inside your eyes.

Touching without trace
Reaching out
But still in place
No promises
No goodbyes
An endlessness
Inside your eyes.

Dorothy Boyd

JUST ME

I am just an ordinary person
    With one or two talents in tow,
My family and friends come first on the list
    Of duties and love to bestow.

Although I am not yet famous,
    Maybe some day I will be,
I really don't care to be anyone else,
    I just want to remain me.

The way that I would plan my day,
    If you should wish to know how,
Is rise at seven, dispense with the chores,
    Then write to 'Poetry Now'.

Barbara Shepherd

THOSE LITTLE EYES
(Dedicated to any mummy and daddy)

There are little eyes upon you,
And they're watching night and day.
There are little ears that quickly,
Take in every word you say.
There are little hands all eager,
And a little girl who's dreaming,
Of the day she'll be like you.

You're the little girl's idol,
You're the wisest of the wise.
In her little mind, about you,
No suspicions ever arise.
She believes in you devoutly,
Believes in all you do or say.
Holds that all you, say and do.
She will say and do in your way
When she grows up like you.

There's a wide-eyed little girl
Who believes you're always right
And her ears are always open
And she watches day and night.
You are setting an example,
Every day in all you do.
For the little girl who's waiting,
To grow up to be like you.

D B Small

HIS MOTHER'S WAR

Those eyes that first beheld him scan the khaki tide, that swirls
with countless mothers' tears and swells with fathers' pride.

The arms that gently held him ache in memory of the years,
for all the tears she rocked away, along with childish fears.

Within the breast that nursed him grieves a lonely heart,
for all the secrets left unshared throughout the years apart.

Oh, not for this she bore him. Or neither did she toil that
war might steal her son away to fight on foreign soil.

The ceremony over, the National Anthem sang,
she seeks the boy she knew so well, but finds instead a man.

He stoops to gently hold her, and she sees with a mother's eyes,
the cord that once had bound them wasn't broken, just untied.

Loraine Darcy

FEAR IS ...

Fear is a large velvety blackness with curious legs,
Fear is standing on a steep crevice, waiting for death's hands.
Fear is being abandoned by the world and waiting for a kind voice.
Fear is suffocation, being held in a vice-like grip by desperate walls.
Fear is being shut in darkness and hearing the scattered gravel clatter on the
                cold wood,
Fear is being trapped between Heaven and Hell, wondering which one
                will call.
Fear is the feel of cold waves dragging you beneath the evil throes of
                seaweed's breathless ride.
Fear is being enticed by curling black smoke and smelling the odour of
                scorched flesh, crying with agony.
Fear is approaching the white light then it fades away so you have to face
                the fears you tried to escape from once again.

Kerry Pickett (14)

GYRATIONS

To see the trees begin to bud each year
To see the stars and planets far and near
We surely must deduce the one true end
That God exists and loves us as a friend.
Yet twixt the trees and planets much we see
Of hunger, torture, sin and misery.
We ask ourselves was our conclusion right
Or just the limitation of our sight . .
A straw to grasp in life's confusing flood
So loathe are we to flounder in the mud.
Copernicus was called a heretic,
He found an answer to what 'makes things tick' -
Then scientific research into nature
Did add much more unto our mental stature.
We need no straws now so well can we swim
We face the truth, no longer pray to him.
We may not fully understand the atom,
But then at least we know that we can split 'em!
When we are asked 'How came this all about?'
'We just don't know,' we angrily all shout.

We know enough right now to get us there -
But like a child again, we ask 'Where's there?'

George Raymond Howarth

WATER

Have you ever given any thought
About the water that you use?
Where do we get the water to drink
That's as instant as we choose?

Water is needed every day
In everything we do
To wash our hands, to wash our hair
Even to flush our loo!

We turn on our taps quite lightly
Just to clean our teeth
And as the water gushes out
It just wastes away beneath

And just think of all the gallons
To fill your bath up to the brim
One quick soak, then it drains away
Surely it could be used again?

You could use all that soapy water
To wash your windows or your car
Or try to find another use
To make your water go twice as far!

You use water to make a cup of tea
And water is used to brew beer
Water can be carbonated
Or purified and clear

We couldn't live without water
As we use it again and again
So next time the sky is cloudy
Just thank God for all the rain!

Sharon Goldsmith

THE EVACUEE

We came from war-torn cities,
A frightened little band;
We all had nametags on our coats
And gas masks in our hand.

Mum told us we'd be safer,
Dad said it was OK
But how could we hope to settle
So many miles away?

Our train was met by Jim and Ann,
A friendly, happy pair;
We saw green fields and cows and sheep,
A world so different there.

They treated us just like their own,
They gave us love and hope.
They helped us write long letters home,
They kept our spirits up.

We grew to love these people
Who helped us through the war.
They opened up their homes and hearts.
Who could have asked for more?

Across the miles and down the years
We've always kept in touch.
Their family and ours are joined
Because they gave so much.

Linda Fleming

MY HOPE

Each night I hope and pray,
That in my arms you'll stay;
I have to share you with another.
But surely that won't be forever,
I love you more than words explain,
But sometimes in our love comes pain,
My love gets complicated -
I don't understand.
There's one thing I have to say,
That is we will never be as one,
I love you 'til the end of time
And that's a long, long time.
I'd like to share my life with you,
But, as you say,
You don't want to be in love with one.
You're like a butterfly, lost, in a garden of make-believe
Here stands a flower,
A real flower of a rose, just for you!
Come, my darling, and live as one,
My dearest one.

W Switzer

A DAWN JOG

I have heard the call of the sun and the sea,
(Sleep on, my dear, I'll turn the key).
I must go where the tide runs free
To bathe in the rising sun.

Down the stair and out of the door,
Past the school and down to the shore.
Maker of all, I Thee adore
As I face the rising sun!

On virgin sand alone I stride,
Fresh as the air and free as the tide.
Chasing the wind with arms flung wide
I embrace the rising sun!

I thank the Lord, as I leave the bay
For the outstretched sand and the salt-sea spray
And the gift of life and another day
To exult in the risen sun!

John Thornton

UNTITLED

The ice which calms the fire
became an object of desire.
Subduing one area of feelings
only to fan another emotion.
As a caring thought sends ideas reeling
the heart beats in rhythm to the ocean.
Soothing balms only inflame
the secret illusion of pain.
Anger flares succeeding in quelling
passion to gentle appreciation
which flourishes, swelling
once questionable elation.
Dreams lay frozen in the eyes
reflecting perfect azure skies.
Reaching out for the shimmering
magic which cools terrible doubts.
Only one last fragment glimmering
in the dancing light, lingers about.
Gathering ashes, rising high
leaving its bounds never to die.

Angus

SPORTING LIFE

'Finney was better than Matthews.'
'No, Matthews had more skill.'
'Yes, but Finney scored more goals.'
'Aye, but Matthews won a Cup Winner's medal.
'That's nothing, Finney played more times for England.'

'Let's ask Ted what he thinks.'
'Hey Ted who was the best Matthews or Finney?'
'Neither of 'em were fit to tie Wilf Mannion's bootlaces.'

'Queer devil that Ted. Can't see anyone's point of view
but his own.'
'I'll agree with you there mate.'

Paul Kelly

MYSTERIOUS MOUNTAIN

The darkness of the scudding cloud
gathers and forms a misty shroud
then drapes it around the mountain top,
cloaks the domineering shape of solid rock
jagged rock outcrops, shadowy shapes
giant figures in grey black capes

the clouds roll by into the night
exposing the highest peaks tipped with white
a spark in the darkness a solitary star
shines at the summit
of the mysterious mountain
viewed from afar.

Joan Chadwick

PEACE OF MIND

I found that I had badly judged
What retirement would really mean
I was in a void of inactivity
Not particularly liking the scene.

At first I read all I could find
Newspapers, books, poems, most anything
But, my brain seemed to want more and more
My thoughts were aloft on the wing.

Waking up in the small quiet hours
I had dreamt about far away lands
Where adventure beckoned all the time
From frozen north to palm dotted sands.

Then, an idea occurred to me
Should I write about my dreams
So that others can enjoy my travels
Masquerading by these means?

Now, I roam the world's surface
I still read to my heart's desire
And in bed or in my old armchair
My dreams are all I desire.

This is one of the poems I've contrived
To explain my glorious peace of mind
Far better than watching an office clock
Dreaming of adventures I'll surely find.

R Nield

I NEVER KNEW YOU LOUIS COHEN

Friday came
Now it won't be the same
The letter page
Has lost its sage.

The content was short
But full of thought
A point well made
And well displayed.

A lively mind
Rarely unkind
As his care shone through
For me and you.

And now his word
Cannot be heard
The words we seek
He cannot speak.

When time has passed
And then we look
We'll find his words
In Heaven's Book.

Tony Sheldon

FOR A CHILD

Said the child,
Why have you done this to me?
Said the adult,
My aim was somewhere else,
But you were in the way.

Mark Craster-Chambers

A NEW AGE

If the common ground of thought
could be broken
by the persistent searchers
a new outlook
a brand new world
will be spawned
and the corpses of western greed
will be scattered
across the doomed cities
preconceived conceptions
of material gains
will diminish
when the energy levels are sufficient
a new age will dawn.

Paul McMullen

RICOCHET

Everything I do always comes back.
I'm a ball in a game of squash.
All originality I lack.
Even my boring thoughts go awash.

Can't think of something new,
my feelings looked on with disgrace.
In the sewer I'm the sew.
I'm simply out of place.

Being me is hard enough.
But, me thinks thoughts are impossible.
I'm just a cart of dusty stuff.
I'm simply repossessible.

Alexander Southgate (13)

CROSSING THE RIVER STYX

Every value
I ever
held
was undermined
my
security
was destroyed,
for
never before
had I seen
death
strike.
Lying there
hands
crossed
just
the
outer shell
the
husk,
I felt
all my
preconceived
ideas
abandon me
as I looked
upon
your
cold face.

Ruth H Davis

SAILING

I hung my soul from a twisted tree
when the sun consumed the oyster moon.
The braying donkey choked in the sea,
dreaming of angel wings that beat way his gloom.

I set sail in my sieve of hopes; my sail-soul
billowed above me. Below my bow, the field
foamed in a storm of birds, their goal
the violet haze of a line the horizon unreeled.

The moon was disgorged: a coppery red trail
across sky blackened for my odyssey of love,
as the clouds spat poisoned fish like hail
to taint my quest: silver fins from above.

The birds wailed their mermaid songs,
while the wind whipped my sole sail to tatters,
lashed to its olive mast. I saw my heart that longs
for you, rip past: flotsam that no longer matters.

The sun-baked earth, my boat, hopes diminished,
was breaking up on the red froth of lanced trust.
The yellowed goat's pus eye leered; it is finished.
Yet, with no soul, no heart, still for you I search. I must.

Norma Winearts

JAM TOMORROW

They used to fill our heads with dreams of how one day robots would
leave us all more leisure time by taking over the workplace and
making fortunes for us. The promised Utopia, however, never
materialised. It seems we were lied to? Or, perhaps, our rotten
masters have grown too fond of easy money to keep their word?

Philip Johnson

THE LIFE WITHIN . . .

To those who fly, to those who walk
To those who wriggle, and those who talk,
To those who breathe, and those who live -
Are all God's creatures, so respect I'll give.
To those with fur, to those with skin
To those who have a life within,
To those of the sky, to those of the earth -
Each life unfolds at the moment of birth.
To those who live with us, to those now extinct
To those of the ocean, which make us think,
To all of those with skin; fur or feather -
On this oasis in space: let's live together . . .

Richard Miller

NEVER LOOK BACK

Never look back in anger
Or forward with too much haste.
Never save time for worry,
Never leave time to waste.
Let dreams be your beginnings
And action be your end.
Let loyalty be your aim,
Then truth be your friend.

Never let hate into your life
And eat away your soul.
Only let love be your light
And honesty be your goal.
Let children be your learning
With the innocence that they give
Then grab hold of life with both hands,
Thank God and then just live.

Paul Atherton

THE WATCHER

I sometimes wonder as I sit and watch what marvel
of creative thought can claim a thousand miles
of car-jammed, street-lamped roads are worth
a million gallons of acid rain.

Progress is a glorious thing, within its graces
lurk inner-city squalor and countryside pollution;
tainted drinking water and improving revolutions.

I love to watch this recycling trend, and have to admit
to glee, when by some unforeseen monetary mishap two tons
of broken glass slip from the collector's grasp, deposited
to miss the tip and smash into a 200 year old tree.

Mice, guinea pigs, monkeys and fluffy rabbits all have
a better life, freed from experimental pain. Progress
means that profit is the thing. Money first. Experiment
after the wonder-drugs are withdrawn. Cheap compensation.

And what of the mighty denizens of your oceans? Treasured
seas? Hunt them to extinction and let rusty tankers
bleed: spread like a carnivorous amoeba.

Could I ever have devised such horrors as man inflicts
upon himself and everything about him? I sit and watch.
I watch and learn the lack of depth in my depravity.

Once it was my lot, fallen from grace, to torment and
tease . . . but now humankind is more adept at these. So,
I just sit and watch. Watch and wonder: just who is the
real tormentor and who is really tormented?

Christine Thomas

WRECKERS

Wreckers we are and wreckers we be,
As you and I look out to sea.
We'll remember that night for evermore,
When we lost our lives for whisky galore.

The night had been dark and full of shadows,
If we were caught it meant the gallows,
We waited long, we waited still
As the beacon blazed atop of the hill.

We saw her coming round the Sound,
Lure her over rocks and run her aground,
Spill her cargo, collect our booty
Free and easy, we paid no duty.

All of a sudden, down on the shore
Custom men firing, a hundred or more
Liquor and blood mixed on the waves,
The fateful night we were sent to our graves.

We knew the risks, we plundered on
Death overtook us, those days are gone,
For wreckers we are, and wreckers we be
Wandering souls for eternity.

Shirley A Woods

THE PERFECT LOVE

When you speak to me my heart explodes
You're the perfect guy I love you loads
The way you smile, the way you talk
I remember when we went for a quiet walk
It was summertime the weather was hot
I want you badly I like you a lot.

Clare Thompson (15)

SHOOTING STAR

Outside their sector,
Out of control,
Heat shields off and all defences down,
Fleeing the interstellar war,
They surfaced near a planet,
At the galactic perimeter,
And as the systems failed,
Inexorably were sucked down,
Racing into an alien, oxygen air,
Screaming their prayers and last despairs,
All roasted live inside the burning shell,
Down on the surface gazing from afar,
Two lovers pledged upon the shooting star.

Ed Blundell

A VISION
(Written before the atom bomb)

I stirred the dying embers to a flame,
And saw a vision of tumult, war and pain.
With increasing horror the vision grew,
Until at last the meaning I knew.
Here were not men I saw before me,
But Satan's devils in high glee.
Then in their place were saddened features,
Frightened children, like haunted creatures.
Their torments knew no bounds,
Echoing hell with their weird sounds.
Surely such a mould could not be,
Man, whose image God made like He.

Eva Lilian Hewertson

WORDS

They can cushion the harshest news.
Soften a bitter blow.
If spoken with understanding and gentleness, they show
The depths of our compassion
Plus the measure of our love.
At times of inner conflict
When one cannot rise above a feeling of desperation
When self-esteem is low
Words can lift a troubled spirit
And make the demons go.
They can mirror thoughts
To bring a soul out of deep despair,
Be equally, when used with spite,
Can help to put it there.
Cruel words can fester like a wound
Causing a hurt so deep
That time will never fully heal
And memory will keep.
A word once spoken out in wrath -
Selected to cause pain -
Can never be retracted:
It nestles in the brain.
It may hide well in daylight
But then, when night is black
The bitter word awakens.
Unwelcome, it comes back.
Consider then, throughout the path of life,
The words are there.
We need them to reach each other.
But handle them with care.

Christina Anglesea

MY BOSS WAS AN OK BOSS - SOMETIMES

In the very first week at the Poly,
It was clear my boss was a wally.
He solemnly averred
We'd to believe every word.

He'd just come back from the States
Where the Miami Herald relates
A store's checkout is manned by The King.
So Jack *knew* Elvis was alive and kicking.

Another tale told to his staff one day
Concerned his prowess and ability to play
Against sportsmen his betters by seed,
But by far his inferiors in deed.

Jack challenged the champion darts player in Sale
The winner to be given a yard of ale.
Needless to say, Jack carried the match
With a six-inch rusty nail and narry a scratch.

Staff meetings are far less inspiring
Now Jack's gone on to a more fitting thing.
He's acting part-time officer I/C,
The local brewery's best publicity.

Roy Lee-Faulkner

MARY

'The colours are not all used up,' she said,
her ninety years dipping and drifting
like friable cast-offs
dropping from October trees
through the no-air day;

breathless, she urges her steps forward
splayed feet shuffling shoals of leaves
crumbling in the crucible of senility.

The Retirement Home have dressed her
in blue and mauve and pink;

soon, serpent-like, she will slough off
the summer-shaded skin;

dust to dust, she alchemises
her geriatric no-life,

and, as the sparks fly upward,
glinting and glancing
in the rays of the sun,
she seems to rise and take her place
dancing among the flame and gold,
potent, in a company of colour.

Angela Butler

IN LIMBO

(An attempt to put into words the effect of severe sensorineural (nerve) deafness)

No bird sings, nor ticking clock,
No sweet music plays, except in memory;
There I conjure up old songs, well loved,
And sometimes scraps of music the mighty Mozart wrote
Will haunt me as I spend my day -
But no bird sings.

Planes scream overhead
And traffic roars until I cringe away.
Unintelligible voices shout
And loud drumbeats assault my ears,
But no bird sings.

In my head are noises no-one else can hear,
Whining, ringing, exploding
Impossible to escape,
How to bear them, oh Lord, at dead of night
When no bird sings.

No sigh of wind in moving trees
Or hum of bees among the flowers;
The stream runs silent on the stones,
Dry twigs snap soundless underfoot,
And no bird sings.

Rene Schofield

RED MEN OF CUMBRIA

The cage is up, the gate slides back
The red men all alight
Shading their brows and squinting their eyes
Against the bright sunlight

Underground all day they toil
Bringing up the ore
Working the seams to find a rich vein
Sweat oozing from every pore.

There's danger there in that dark world
An ever present foe
When a pit prop moves and the roof caves in
Burying the men below

At the pit top they stand in silence
They wait all night and day
Mothers, wives and sweethearts
All they can do is pray

Now the cage wheel stands like a monument
To remind us all each day
Of the brave red men who once mined there
A pittance for their pay

Glenda Greeson

UNFORGETTABLE

Still she smiles in my mind,
Such tender love
The unforgettable kind.
Long ago, happy days,
Till we'd to move
Our separate ways.
A nugget from life's goldmine.
She was eight, me nine.

William Dover

OAP (OLD, ALONE, PERSON)

Alone, afraid, a voice unheard
Like a dictionary without a word
Encased in a body which doesn't belong
Frustrated just like a flightless bird
Tired and weary, not easily stirred
A lifetime's reward, for doing no wrong?

Bright beckoning light shines, yet I cannot go
Inner feelings, becoming difficult to show
Each passing moment, each movement I make
A silent victory, for in my heart I know
Beneath this, is myself, hidden below
My unforgiving exterior, the pain I must take

Your pity, forgive me, I do not wish to receive
Simply respect my dignity, for I want to believe
My life has a meaning, I pray to be heard
Physically, I realise, I can never retrieve
All that has passed - alas don't let me deceive
For every word I utter is a heartfelt word.

Lisa Jones

BYGONE DAYS

Eeh! I never thought there'd ever be a day,
Always knew, and thought, we'd barter just to have our say,
Closing the pit, they can't, tests showed and proved to all of us,
At least a 150 years' coal seams, lying ready, why all this fuss?
The government, they know nowt, call the union, they'll sort it out,
They can't? The others, they'll back us to the hilt, they won't?
We held out on strike, many a time, for their causes, didn't we?
Our lass, and bairns, did without for weeks on end, don't tell me,
A slap in the face, they don't want to know,
No more riding the belt outby, trying to catch the first cage home,
Get me out before Ken, I'll swing for it, when he finds out what I've done,
They closed the colliery, next one down to us, and they say,
It will be only a matter of time, before it's us, just another day,
I'll get along home and shovel in the coal, it's an eyesore,
Our lass will be truly mad, if I don't get it done afore four,
Na, na, I can't I've got to tend to the garden, and me tomato plants,
I can't, I can't, our lass wants to go to the club's fifties dance,
Que sera, what will be, will be, on their heads be it,
I'm sick of fighting through mud and water, each and every shift,
Sick to the teeth of airless, tight, dark and gloomy crypt,
That's what it is, beneath this sea bed, desolate,
By man, and tools, raped and ravaged, truly desecrated,
Boxing clever, those government people, for electricity and gas,
Shut us down, they've done it before, what is their purpose?
To line their pockets, sell us out cheap, I've seen it all before,
They can't kill our community as easily as that, they don't know the score,
We look after each other, they will never understand that,
Never no-one behind you, ready to stab you in the back,
They've never had, or will have, even know where to begin,
We'll stand together, forever, through thick and thin.

Shirley Atkinson

ASPIRATIONS

I look into the mirror
The image is the same.
But where's the girl from yesterday
Before this letter came?

My eyes are burning brighter,
My skin a glowing pink.
My body straighter standing
At least six foot, I think.

Reports of this achievement
I'll shout it round the town.
Sing it from the roof tops
I'll broadcast up and down.

I can't believe my fortune
An end to doubts and fears.
No longer a no-hoper,
Success in later years.

You see today I heard the news
My poem's now in print.
My self-esteem has rocketed
My heart begun to sprint.

So all you struggling poets,
Whose attempts are met with mirth . .
Ply your trade, with head held high
One day you'll prove your worth.

C Sue Appleton

THE RACE IS ON

The race is on the gallop of the horses as each one runs by
with tails outspread behind him his eyes look straight ahead.
As his jockey strokes his head, 'Come on now my beauty we'll soon be
home and dry, but first of all I need you now so just give it a try.'
With nostrils all a flaying and foam around the jaws you give one more
jerk and run, soon the cup is yours.
The sound it's like a battle as everyone does cheer, but most of all it's over
when you hear them roar.
You beat the fillies to the ground even the black could run

                                   behind you no more.
So there my beauty now you've won.
Thank you for what you've done.

Elizabeth A Wilkinson

WILLIAM SMILED

William smiled at me today
and now my heart is glad.
It is a trivial thing to say,
meant nothing to the child,
and yet, I'm certain, William smiled.

William does not always smile.
His days are black, then white.
He lay and whimpered for a while,
this baby soft and mild,
but still, I'm certain, William smiled.

William came upon the world
a mere two months ago.
From dark to light he has been hurled;
his thoughts are vague and wild
and yet, I know, he smiled.

Gill Pomfret

COLLIDING COLLISIONS

There's collision
of thoughts
with actions.

Limitations
intervening
with determination.
Obstacles
appearing
and clear paths
disappearing.

But I know
Optimism is elite,
And it leaves pessimism
In defeat.

And I know
To be strong,
Is better
Than to be weak.

And I know
Someday
my thoughts and actions
will go hand in hand,
And
Be equal,
Be true
To my mind's sequel.

Humera Khan (17)

TIME CHANGES ALL THINGS

Once, I craved peace and solitude, whilst
Pop music's plangent beat pulsed inside my head
Like an alien heart, perpetrators oblivious.
Bedrooms reeled from the shock of constant onslaught.
Grubby T-shirts and socks lay undisturbed in dark places.
My Hoover would grind to a halt, quivering in fear
As I tried to force it from the safety of the landing,
Into the rooms where *they* slept, the doors a demarcation
Line between normality and insanity.
Stairs groaned under the constant weight of strangers
Who drifted - phantomlike - in a never ending procession.
Surely, only *two* were mine?
In *their* presence, things would mutate,
Light switches developed a will of their own,
And refused to exist in the off position.
Spinning record decks attained perpetuity.
In the bathroom, tidemarks adorned bath and washbasin,
Toothpaste tubes searched in vain for lost tops.
Towels hung damp and listless, beaten into submission
By hands, hastily *washed* en route to *going out.*
Doors banged ferociously, or gaped like toothless mouths,
Gulping in the cold night air.
However . . . time changes all things.
Today tidiness reigns supreme.
Empty bedrooms rest in peace.
The silence is deafening - and my heart aches
For children who are now men!

Penny Daniels

VIKINGS

They came from another age,
With axe and shield,
Turned every village,
Into a battlefield

From their leader a war cry
The swords at the ready
The eagles take to the sky,
Wondered how they missed me.

I crawled into their camp,
Dagger of mine don't let me down.
My hand with sweat grew damp,
As the leader took off his plundered crown.

I shook off my pursuers,
Travelling on my own now,
Through trees of beech and firs,
I'll make the next village somehow.

You've been taken to task
By many a one,
But behind that mask,
You hide a gun,
All you could save
Was needless wrath
And over your grave,
There'll be no epitaph!

Mille V

THE FLOWER

I plant a seed.
Then watch it grow.
I see the flowers
Come and go.
The colours glow.
So very bright
All through the day
And through the night
I watch it bloom
Then slowly die
Another season has passed us by.

C Whitehead

LIFE

I woke to look at my life
That was so very dear.
Life so full of pain and fear
But that is life.

Out of the dark came light,
My light was so very bright.
A dream came true a dream untrue,
But that is life.

I held a rose in my hand,
My rose I did not understand
My rose was mine and mine alone,
Never more to be on my own.

I wish I could say what is in my heart,
The words won't come,
Where do I start.
But that is life.

Margaret Ann Rogerson

MY JOURNEY

When I'm an old lady,
I'll sit and dream of things that's been,
Of summer days when I was young,
Of cornfields yellow and fields of green,
As on life's journey I'd just begun

Of pearls and pictures and memories kept,
Deep inside my treasure chest,
Of lace and satin, ribbons and silk,
Lips of red and skin of milk,
Of golden hair and eyes of blue,
My journey now is halfway through.

I've loved and lost my precious things,
Of babies' toys and wedding rings,
But deep inside my treasure chest,
Hair now of grey and eyes to rest,
I pick out one memory I treasure the best
My love for you I keep and tend,
As now my journey is near the end.

M Benson

LOVE

What is it?
Is it a sense, a feeling,
Can we see it, or feel it?
Do we all have it?
It could be an act of kindness
A gesture a smile a touch
An unexpected message a gift
It's powerful recognise it and receive it.

J Campbell Jones

TO ANGIE IN AMERICA

I received a phone call today
From someone very far away
From a lady I like to call a friend
And I hope to until the end.
We don't correspond as much as we should
But when we do the feeling's good.
Her phone call was such a surprise
And I must confess
It brought tears to my eyes
So, whenever I'm feeling blue
I remember that voice
And think of you - Angie.

J Bradshaw

EYE OF THE BEHOLDER

They say beauty is in the eye of the beholder.
When the eye of the beholder glances at the woman I love.
He will see a figure heavenly designed.
Eyes that are crystal clear.
Skin so beautiful you cannot help but want to caress it.
A smile that can thaw a heart of ice.
A Goddess.
She could charm ten thousand men with a single glance.
With those clear deep eyes, she would be able to
persuade men to walk into hell, they would willingly,
for just one brush of her dark red lips on their
cheeks.
If God was trying for perfection he created it in
the woman I love.

Allan Toothill

TIME GOES BY

They stand together marked with age,
the master and the shire.
The youth goes past with smoke,
and noise, not much to their desire.

Long years have passed since they first strode,
together in the fields, working the ground,
while all around, the earthy smells, and birds
as well, sang as they went along.

All the progress through the years, with pleasant
things to do, ploughing, sowing, reaping, mowing,
just to name a few. Now they stand and view the
land, some time remaining still.

Tractors roaring round the fields,
wireless playing loudly, ridges sown,
crops are mown, tankers spreading,
mowers tedding, all as time goes by.

Systems come and systems go, as country
folk know well, but in a hundred years,
who knows? But only time will tell.

Peter Isles Orr

HIT MAN

The night was dark
The stars shone bright
The cold bit deep
No-one is sight
His blade was sharp
And sure his hand
His victim soon was
In the promised land

Philip Corbishley

SUPERMAN AND LOIS LANE (ON TV)

I suppose it had to happen:
The moment Lois realised Clark Kent
Was Superman in specs.

How she could fail to see
Their equalled physicality
Defied belief.
We knew of course,
Had known the secret
From the start,
Voyeurs to his quick-change dash,
As yet again, he saved the world
Or Lois, from some catastrophic doom.
Every Superman must look the part:
The logo worn across the heart,
No laddered tights
In uniform of red and blue,
The stance that says -
I'm honest and I'm true.

Before computers - comic books:
We cruised imagination's internet,
Dreaming of flight.

Now adult preoccupations
Stalk us,
We fear pick-pockets
In crowded places,
Suspicious of faces
We do not know.
We waver at the pavement edge,
Waiting for the lights to change,
Half hoping for Superman.

Corinne Hedgecock

YOU

You are the flame in the
heart of my burning desire,
you are the blood
that warms my whole being,
you are the scent
that lingers on my pillow,
you are the light in my soul
that will never go out,
you are the melody
that charms my ears,
you are the trigger
that fires my senses,
you are the solid wall
that I can lean upon,
you are the mystery tour
that takes me to paradise,
you are the daydream
that caresses my thoughts,
you are the waterfall
in my secret garden,
you are the sweetest song
from the tiny birds at dawn,
you are the sunshine
that illuminates my darkest hour,
you are the ticking of the clock
every second that I miss you,
you are all around me
every hour of every day, and
you are the one
that I cannot live without.

Victoria Cropper

AUNTIE PEEP

You've been with us for many a year,
And in our hearts you've become very dear.
You've been there with love and support,
We always knew you to be a good sport.
When we were ill or someone made us cry,
You calmed us and soothed us with a story or a lullaby,
You've given relations and friends lots of hours of pleasure
So we've lots of memories of you, to recall and treasure.
Our great loss, is God's gain,
And in our hearts you will remain.
For you have been one of the best,
So take it easy, put up your feet and God bless.

Catherine Ainscough

THE MAN WITH THE A4 PAD

I watched him sitting solo, by the sea.
His handsome face so tanned, appealed to me.
His slender hands, his slightly greying hair.
The sea-breeze stirred the A4 pad on which he scribbled there,
So intent - so feverishly he wrote.
(Was he a budding novelist, thinking and remote?)
But then the page wafted off his knee
And landed at the feet of Nosy Me!
I picked it up and glanced at what he'd written . . .
A long long list beginning -
Bread - potatoes - cat food -
(How I wished I were his kitten!)

Marjory Baker

MY BEST FRIEND

I have a friend who thinks I am
Some special sort of Superman
She never says I drive too fast,
Or tells me I am getting past,
The age for rolling on the mat,
She never says 'You're getting fat.'
She never says my jokes are boring,
Or wakes me up if I am snoring,
She does not mind how long she waits,
When I go boozing with my mates,
I know her love will never fail,
She's watching me now,
And wagging her tail.

Fred A Robertson

MY MAM

To the best Mam in the land
She was always there to understand
To cook my meals
And wash my clothes
How she managed God only knows
When it was time for me to go out
She had ironed my shirt
And laid it out
I had nothing to do
Because she had even cleaned my shoes
Going home to the one who cares
Because I knew she would always
Be there

B Barnett

MOONLIGHT

As I looked to the sky
One moonlight night
I saw! What to me
Was a wonderful sight
The moon like a ball
So white and clear
Not a cloud in sight
Not a breath of air
The calm sea beneath
Like a pond or a lake
This is God's earth
His hands helped to make
What do you see
Oh! Moon up there
As you look down on the earth so bare
It is only by night you come out and shine
Down on this earth
This Island of mine

Margaret Cain

LIFE'S STORY

New times different ages
Life's a book filled with pages
Each person's a story
With heartaches and glory

Chapter 1 Your Identity from the moment you're born
Chapter 2 Is your childhood and the knowledge you learn
Chapter 3 You've decided your goals and aims
Chapter 4 Your commitments possessions and gains
Chapter 5 Is for memories which hold close to your heart
Chapter 6 Your identity makes a final depart

L McCoy

PARADISE?

When people talk of paradise,
I wonder what they mean,
To some,
Paradise is a brilliant sunset,
Or a chocolate chip ice-cream.

But each and every person's thoughts,
Are different and extreme,
It's what separates me from you,
It's a uniqueness that's unseen.

We often find we race through life,
And never stop to think,
There must be more,
Than what we do
From 9 till 5 all week.

The word is not as great as it seems,
To a younger child's eyes
It's not all golden fields of corn,
And perfect clear blue skies.

They don't see the world's confusion,
They don't see the world of fear,
I'm not quite sure where paradise is,
But it certainly isn't here.

Cher Heckle

CAROUSEL

Please let me off this merry-go-round
I've had enough of the ride.
For no-one said it would go so fast
Or hurt so much inside.

Oh! The music was gay as we galloped away
With never a backward glance.
But no-one said 'Get off while you may,
You won't get a second chance.'

Louder and faster the music was played
We had all the fun of the fair.
But suddenly the night grew cold
And you didn't seem to care.

And I looked around for the friends I had lost.
I looked but never found.
And no-one said that was part of the cost
Of the thrills of the fair-ground.

So let me get off this merry-go-round.
Let the songs and the music be still.
For no-one said that your heart could break
When you went on the carousel.

Anita Tomlinson

MARRIAGE

Trudging along grey granite pavements,
Windswept, weary, and both hands heavy
With shopping bags, suitcases, bad debts, bitterness,
And round each turning another emotional levy.

Opening the front door onto colour and carpet
The pressure falls away from my aching spine;
A sofa, hot tea, chocolate, patience, care -
Still here, thank you, still mine.

Isobel Ridley

THE DIVER

He stands, tall and strong in his shiny black suit,
adjusts his mask,
concentrates his mind on the immediate task,
straps on his air tank, checks the pressure,
opens the valve, not too wide,
He's ready now and over the side,
He's falling, he's sinking, he's going down
to the ocean bed, a watery town,
a place of shadows and golden lights
where earthly troubles and earthly plights
are banished and ended once and for all
by a waving plant or a coral wall.
It's so beautiful there, so peaceful and calm,
a place where his soul can come to no harm,
where he drifts along at the slowest pace
and the fish come up and poke at his face,
It's a world full of wonder, where he can discover
all manner of things, the sea's like a lover
caressing him gently with whispering sighs,
and starfish are jewels before his eyes
and sea horses wave in tender motion,
He's found his world at the bottom of the ocean.

Audrey Johnston

OF A THOUSAND DAYS AND NIGHTS

I lay and I dream of a thousand days.
I see him charge in to unleash his within.
Unwrapping the love from the silken white frame
By full moon and candle. Comes rise and comes fall.
That satin white smell of magnolia flesh mingled
With shimmering nights of honeysuckle love.
His love words like raindrops fall heavy from full lips
And settle and simmer on hot, willing skin.

I lay and I dream of a thousand nights,
Where we creep in like thieves to steal from inside.
First with a gentleness to drink from love's pool
And then with a boldness to reap the reward.
Then coming together is soon torn apart
And the prince, once with princes, is now crowned a king.
Unveiling his conquest, he leaves now in silence -
His legacy of valour relinquished within.

My dreams are of thousands upon thousands more,
That in the cold daylight fade into the mist.
Go walking in clouds, bathed in sunlight's rays new.
'Til the dawn yields to dusk, just as she yields to you.

Kate Roddis

NORTH WEST FOREVER

Residents of the North West are we,
Even though we've travelled the world to see
Many different cultures all around
But none to match the North West we have found.

The industrial town of Oldham, the place of our birth,
Where we loved, married, had children and enjoyed such mirth.
Then over to Blackpool to continue our life,
With many joys but alas much strife.

Now we are over 60 years,
Grandparents and pensioners with lots of fears.
The great North West is still our home,
Even though when we win the lottery we long to roam.

People born and bred in the great North West,
Will always remain loyal till they're laid to rest.
Living their lives the best way they can,
Returning as always from whence they have ran.

Christine F Maule

THE HILL

The ageing hill
Stood still

Fields grassing
Time passing

Fences corroding
Weather eroding

Ramblers ambling
Lambs a'gambolling

Lovers loving
Earth moving

Rain saturating
Rocks disintegrating

Yet the hill
Stands still.

Jennifer Taylor

ANGUISH

You are an unnecessary interruption to my life,
I don't know why I ever became your wife,

If only I'd known when I was younger,
What it would be like to live with an amoeba,
A drunken one at that with no goal or aim,
A lazy one at that you put me to shame,

When you asked me to marry you in those handsome days,
You failed to tell me I'd have to live in a maze
Of confusion not knowing if you'd kiss me or hit me,
Or hold and caress me or throw something at me,

But you my darling are detachable,
Not like my happiness that's indispensable,

So I will detach, divide, subtract, this mental and physical anguish I'm
suffering,
And I'll multiply, increase, satisfy, my desire for the freedom I long to be
experiencing,

But what if I left now without leaving a note for you . . .?
Oh, you probably wouldn't notice for an hour or two,
'Til you found you had no-one to bruise to the bone,
So good-bye my darling I'm not coming home.

Delia Rutlidge

BARGAIN

Every day when you wake it's a bargain,
Whether you realise it or not,
Because today your Giro's landing
Or three numbers on the trot.

The morning rage always a good deal,
It's always full of news
You know what royalty's doing.
And a rare victory for the blues.

How we need power share issues,
With none of the stuff to share,
We could think about profit sharing,
Float yer man at the top of the stair.

The air we breathe it has no value,
For it has no levy or toll,
Fat cats lap up our cream,
And polish their tarnished gold.

Swarm for the sacrificial shopping,
More for want than for need,
You can't barter with the starving
And they can't swallow your greed.

When you lay down your head it's respite
For to get by you're an eight hour ghoul,
To bid you must slave with compliant minds,
To mend the holes in your shoes

G F J

OUR EMILY

Angelic looks and sparkling eyes,
Impish ways they do disguise,
And if there's mischief to be done,
Our Emily's there, she'll be the one.

Such a sweet smile upon that face,
Petite in stature and full of grace,
Yet inside this fairy frame,
Lives a naughty nymph who likes to reign.

Words that sound as sweet as honey,
As she pokes the eye of mummy,
Soft kisses, feathery light,
Until they turn into a bite.

As you help and teach her each day,
She always does it her own way,
There's no telling her what to do,
For Emily will tell you too!

Yet when she's snuggled up asleep in bed,
And you gaze upon her precious head,
You're sure there's a halo shining bright,
Make the most of it, it's only there at night!

Kay Holmes

OH LITTLE ONE!

Oh little child, why do you sit so still?
Oh little child, why do you look so ill?
Oh little one, why are you all alone, on your
Own with no-one to care,
With little to spare?

Why do you stare at the empty walls,
Seeing nothing and feeling nothing?
Why does your head hang limp?
No noise, no movement, are you dead?
But your hand just moved upon the bed.

Oh little child look at me and see, that I feel
For thee.
What can I do, hold you tight?
And give you my loving all through the night.
But it is not loving you need,
It is food to build and help you to breathe with
A little more ease.

But there is no money today for your Dad has
Gone away.
No food may I buy for we have lost our supply.
Your mum is ashamed but it is not me to blame.
Oh little one still love me Son!

Norma Grundy

EARLY MORNING POETRY

Early in the morning it struck 5.30am
With the heartbeat of the night before
Still pounding in my head,
The taste of the night before
Still stale in my mouth
Earlier than I would normally rise
It rises out of
The muddled haze of my head
And calls for paper
And a pen
To track out its life
Across the clean page.
And so I scribble
A slave to poetry
While somewhere outside
The day lurks
In the crisp morning air,
The birds calling
And the people still sleep.

Catherine Makin

THE HUNTER

All hope is gone, nowhere to run, no place to hide.
To face the hunter, trapped at last,
Dark eyes look into the face of man.
What do they see in the last moments of their life?
Do they see the bright red coats like living blood.
Blend with theirs in scarlet hue?
And as they feel the tooth and claw
Do they see in him the savage streak
That lies forever in his dark soul?

Jean Edwards

FAMILY DAY OUT

'Dad, dad, can we have a ninety nine dad?
Mom, can we go to the fair?
Dad, can we have a ride on the donkeys?
Oh! What's going on over there?
Dad, dad, can we go for a paddle?
Can you buy us a bucket and spade?
Can you build us a sandcastle dad?
Bigger than their dad's made?
Dad, dad, where's mom gone?
Has she gone to buy us some rock?
Dad, I've just stood on a jelly fish,
And it's squashed all over my sock!
Dad, dad, come and play football,
We'll let you be Cantona,
We'll be Shearer, Giggs, and Redknapp,
Bet you don't get far.
Dad, dad, look here comes mom,
She's bought us all Fish 'n' Chips,
Look at them two men playing Frisbee, dad,
They look like a right pair of drips.
Mom, mom, what took you so long?
Have you got us a drink?
Guess what! Dad's been eyeing the bikinis
And giving the girls a wink!
Dad, dad, can we stay here?
Do we have to go home tonight?
Mom, dad, it's getting windy,
Can you go and buy us a kite . . .?'

D B Feseto

LIFE GONE BY

There she sits on the moor alone
Just staring out thinking of life gone by

Wrinkled with age of days gone by
A hard life she's had but no more

She's been left on the scrap heap
Too old, gnarled and worn out by work and life

The wind blows her hair
Obscuring her face her tears her life gone by

The moor is green and lush with life
But not her she sits looking but not seeing

She stands and walks a bent figure
But not a sound she makes

She disappears mingled with the landscape
Just a lonely woman thinking of life gone by.

Gillian McFarland

ALL IS NOT WELL IN THE WORLD

Everything's gone so bitter and cold.
Laughter has gone we're all getting old.
Deep down everyone knows it, they don't need to be told.
They toss away their soul for a piece of gold.
Seems like any second this planet will buckle and fold.
They say a thing only has value if it can be sold.
Sitting at home in front of the tube turning to mould.
Where are all the real people vibrant and bold?
Life's spinning too fast the centre can't hold.

Leigh Smith

WELCOME ARRON MARK

I'm sat here wondering what to do
I really want to hear news of you.
Should I ring the hospital or not?
Will they tell me what I've got?
It's been a while and I haven't heard,
Not a phone call, not a word.
My nerves are frayed, I'll have to phone,
There it is the dialling tone.
I'm dialling now, fingers shaking,
A very important call I'm making.
'Hold the line, I'll just find out.'
Something's happened, without a doubt.
The nurse comes back and announces loudly,
I'm sitting here, my head held proudly.
I burst into tears, but tears of joy,
My third Grandchild's arrived.! Yippee, it's a boy.

Denise Clitheroe

THE UPSIDE TOWN

from the Beacon's brow
was a galaxy of lights below.

As dusk elapsed on New Year's Day,
the apertures and time delays
could not expand or give the lie
to that grey template of the sky.

The New Town, lit up, slid indoors,
like a star-flung sea, on broken shores.

Will Daunt

REFLECTION

Mirrors, mirrors
By the wall
Do I really care
What you say at all?
I look to you to see myself
To comment on my mental health
But does your glass
Reflect me true
Or is the image
More of you?

Mirrors, mirrors
Round the table
Trying to shine
As best they're able
Reflecting in each other's glasses
Blending with the drunken masses
What you show
May not be right
But how else do I
Use my sight?

The Adjuster

THE LAKE

A shimmering, rippling surface top
Your movement never seems to stop
With depth and darkness down below
What secrets held? No-one shall know

When winter falls you're deep and cold
Your waters dark and very old
Your beauty there for all to see
This life of yours so pure so free

Upon your banks the trees all stand
Like children watching hand in hand
Your never ending flow of life
Pass by without the slightest strife

In summer time you are alive
With creatures that need you to survive
And people come from round this land
But none could ever understand.

P Radcliffe

UNTITLED

When moonbeams cross
the sky at night
And all the world is still
And owls are calling from
the heights of tall trees
by the mill
'Tis then we think of
days gone by
When all the world
was small
And ladies wore their
hair up high
And did for ribbons call
And then we think of
modern days
And changes which have
passed
And fashions which have
made their ways
And pleased the world at
last.

Ruth Lloyd

STORMY SEAS

Walking by the sea-shore on a stormy winter's day.
Where sands are lashed by angry waves on which white horses play.
The power of these mighty waves is all too plain to see
Like demons from unfathomed depths fighting to be free.
Sturdy sea-walls shudder as the thundering water breaks
Spewing forth into the air to fall as icy flakes,
Carrying upon its back pebbles from the beach
Flinging them like cannon-balls as far as it can reach.
Boats are tossed like corks upon these mighty surging waves
While down below lie mariners lost in watery graves,
The wind whips up a raging fury no man can defy
Dragging down the angry clouds that race across the sky.
Mother nature in her glory tells the world that she
Rules the air, the land and sea, for all eternity.

Elizabeth M Carter

TIME

A soothing expanse of calm
Ripples of sound where sea meets shore
Almost quiet in its giving
But cruel in its taking.

The sea that looks so endless
Has no limit as you seek
Ships on the horizon
But nothing disturbs the peace

Hypnotic the shiver of pebbles
Against the sea shore
The feeling of infinite time
The sea goes on forever

Jeanne Bradley

SHY

Want to heckle. Sit and simmer.
     Wish I dared
     to be heard.
Why is my light always dimmer?
     How absurd.

Stranger joins us. How to greet you?
     Wish I knew
     what to do.
'How d'you do?' or 'Pleased to meet you?'
     That's not true.

Meetings daunt me. Folks are scaring.
     Petrified,
     try to hide.
Joining in is for the daring.
     I'm outside.

Anne Ashworth

SLUMBER

The sun shines differently here,
As havoc and headaches fade away,
The moonlight shines differently here,
As I relax in true awe of the night's beauty,
The sea looks cleaner here,
As I watch the ripples of the tide flow across the shore,
I'm a different person here,
As I welcome the peace and sleep.

Rebecca Keight

LE PONTREAU

There's a small piece of heaven,
on earth, I know,
in a tiny French village
called Le Pontreau.
No television. No telephone.
No traffic to stir you.
You're miles from home.
A cottage with shutters
and ivy clad walls.
A gecko runs out. A young cuckoo calls.
You wake in a morning
No sound can be heard
but the rustle of leaves
and the songs of the birds.
You walk through a gateway
and sit by the stream.
No-one around, except you
and your dream.
The dragonflies hover. The butterflies too
in their bright coloured dresses
which sparkle with dew.
The peace that surrounds you
you cannot compare,
for once you have touched it,
you know that it's there.
There's a small piece of heaven
on earth, I know,
in a tiny French village
called Le Pontreau.

Jeannette Jacobs

A RAMBLER

I'm too big, I'm too fat, or so 'tis said
When I say I'm out walking and not asleep in my bed
But I've walked for years with all this weight
My heart's tested regular, *nowt* wrong with its rate.
I've climbed the hills, I've walked the dales;
Possibly sweat, possibly wailed
But I've come through it all, hell and high water;
I've walked with the skinnies and given no quarter
So, what say you, dieticians, politicians
Should I be in my grave and not with the living?
I say to you all do what you will;
Forget all the fads, ignore all the spiel
Eat what you like within moderation
And thumb your nose to the rest of the nation.

Margaret Charlesworth

LITTLE SWEET PEA

Fragile and pale
       as you sway on the breeze

A rainbow of colours
       as you peep thro' the trees

An aroma so fragrant
       you perfume the air

Pure perfection and beauty
       you nurture with care

So special, exquisite
       you always will be

My most favourite of flowers
       dear little sweet pea

Joan Brookfield

THE OLD LADY NEXT DOOR

I feel really sorry toward the old lady next door,
No-one has time for her, they say she's a bore.
While she eats her digestives and sips her tea,
No-one understands her and only she can see.

Hobbling down the road, old, frail and mellow,
She isn't white anymore but a custard yellow.
It's been a long time since she was last hugged or kissed,
And her unfortunate husband is so sadly missed.

He was seen through the sights of a luger turret,
And shot in the lungs by a jerry's bullet.
Right in the corner she's always sat,
Watching Emmerdale Farm and stroking her cat.

Years ago she must have been a lovely wife,
Before her heartaches, her troubles and strife.
Now she relies on her widow's pension,
And to live peacefully is her main intention.

She has a daughter - God knows where she's at,
She never seems to visit, though there's 'Welcome', on the mat
The vicar on occasions decides to visit,
And a small glass of sherry is about her limit.

Then last week the milk started to accumulate,
And poor Mrs Thompson is now the 'late'.
She never had much and was never mean,
Now of course the daughter is on the scene.

The daughter took everything that she was able,
And now all that is left is the garden bird table.
Above Mrs Thompson's resting place the daughter towers,
To deliver Mrs Thompson her first and last bunch of flowers.

J Boylan

THE RIVER

The soft rain falls on mountain tops
No trees or grass to feed
It seeps into the crevices
Then gathers weight and speed

To cascade over craggy rocks
On ever downwards run
Like silver ribboned rivulets
Clear, sparkling in the sun

When joined by other neighbours, it
Becomes a babbling brook
A winding stream, a gill, a beck,
With ne'er a backward look

Where streams converge, a river's born
Of gorges, falls, and weirs,
Some peaceful stretches in between
With boathouses and piers

The cool, clear water disappears
Through great industrial towns
The soft rains of the mountainside
With filth and mud are drowned

Tidal now as on it flows
Towards the estuary
At journey's end the river goes
To join the open sea

M S Whipp

GRANDMA

Grannie is sitting in her chair,
With silver highlights in her hair.
The lamps are lit, the fire does glow.
Thoughts of the past, start to flow.
When she was young and just a girl
The life she lived, was one big whirl.
She danced and sang the night away.
But, sat and dreamed all the day.
The years went by, she met her fate,
It all began with her first big date
Into a life of romance, she was led
She couldn't wait until she was wed
The children came, oh! double joys
She'd always wanted little boys
They gave her joy, she had such fun.
They certainly had her on the run
First came school, with lots to learn
Then, off to work, to start to earn
The years sped by, she lost them all
Now, there was no-one, wanted to call.
So, she sits and thinks, about her past,
And wonders, how long loneliness will last.

Marianne Ritson

THE DRYSTONE WALL

I am the drystone wall,
by river and by fall,
O'er mountain side and valley deep
the mist embraces me so sweet.

Keep near me when you're walking
I'm like a friend there talking
keep by me and tread this well worn way
you'll be safe if by my side you stay.

I am shelter from the wind and rain,
rest on me while breath you gain.
I am also shade when the weather's hot
I provide that lovely cooling spot.

I am home for animals, moss and fern,
for occasional help to you I turn,
If my stones should fall beneath your feet,
Please pick them up and make them neat.

E G Boyle

A GOD THAT CARES

It's nice to have a God that cares
That does not like the one that swears.
That cares for the things we speak and do
There is no other God like you.
Your thoughts are not our thoughts we know
And yet you love us all the more.
You care if we're happy or if we are sad
And we hurt you so much Lord when we are bad.
You gave us the world a beautiful place
But man keeps on making it a disgrace.
But you dear Father I know in my heart
Will not let man tear it apart.
You sent your Son Jesus down here on earth
To show us the price you thought we were worth.
He spoke of your kingdom and of your great love
And soon he'd return to his Father above.
He suffered so much to pay for our sin
Though only a few hearts he knew he would win.
Yet he was prepared to lie down his life
Oh thank You dear Lord for your great sacrifice
Worthy of Jesus please let me be
But much more dear Father worthy of thee.

M Kay

113

WHEN THE LIGHTS GO ON AGAIN

Towards the end of August in Blackpool,
The time when the illuminations are checked,
Come electricians with light bulbs and ladders
And rolls of new wire, I expect.

There's a growing feeling of excitement
In the lives of the locals, young and old
As they count the days to the switch-on
And the evenings get darker and cold.

The hotels and guest houses fill up
As sightseers arrive for the fun,
With their Kiss-me quick hats and a hot dog
And nobody misses the sun!

The prom is teeming with people
And the roads are crammed with cars.
As usual, the trams and the coaches
Are lit with a myriad of stars.

It's always a night to remember,
Five miles of twinkling lights,
In colours that defy description,
One of England's most breathtaking sights.

And when they switch off in November
With the visitors having gone home,
Blackpool will plan for the next one
Which leads me to finish my poem.

Jon Ayling

LOVE POEM FROM THE MOORS

You are my rock.
You stand tall, and firm, and steady, and shelter me
from all the corrosive rain that eats the world.
And whilst you harbour me, the acid trickles down,
making furrows of your soul.
I am the grass.
I quiver in the wind and gently tickle you, and
make you laugh.
From nothing, I have rooted in your crevices
and grown my strength.
The rock stands huge against the storm,
But the grass is tenacious and clings on forever
Until they are as one.
Interwoven sanctuary.

J P Pedder

FRUSTRATION

Trapped behind the bars of this mortal body
Is caged the soul of an athlete,
A sportsman determined and strong
Who once burst from the starting blocks
Like a well-bred stallion
To lead those in awe breathless and weak
A player's player
Whose muscle and sinew was deemed infallible,
A leader, protector and king
Yet as with kings of days gone by
Those not in awe would boil, in envy
So when in battle this warrior fell
Muscle and sinew torn away,
His subjects simply took his mace
As a thousand men could take his place.

Michael A Jackson

STOP THE WORLD

Stop the world, I wanna get off.
I just won't be a pawn in your game.
Go to war, kill and die, but do we truly know why?
Can't you see, we're all going insane?

Do you ever take time to ponder my friend,
On the hell we are being led into?
They are stealing our minds, ruling our lives,
Don't shake your head, 'cos it's happening to you!

'Doctor, I need you, got this pain in my head.'
'Now don't fret, take these pills, go to bed.'
Yes, drugs may be the answer, oh, but what is the cure,
For the countless who are now lying dead?

We build nuclear weapons to destroy fellow men,
When so many are starving and poor.
Spending billions on death, oh, but why not on life,
Or does no-one see sense anymore?

Look, look around you at the beauty.
Listen, please listen to your soul.
What will we leave for the children,
When the earth is but a Black Hole?

'Let there be peace!' is the cry of our world.
Oh, you hypocrites, all leaders on Earth!
How dare you to speak of love and goodwill,
With corruption and hate in your heart.

So, stop the world, I have to get off.
I just can't be a pawn in this game.
Go to war, kill and die, will we ever know why?
Don't you see? . . . We're already insane.

Zona Addylyn

SPRING

Oh lovely spring
When nature stands renewed
And each day brings
Fresh sights of beauty rare
When budding hedgerows
Greet the morn bedewed
And songbirds trill
Their sweet notes in the air
What fine and stately home
Could ever own
A carpet such
As mother nature weaves
What artist match
The colour or the tone.
Of the beauteous flowers
Of springtime and the leaves.

What builder ever worked
With skill and zest
The way the feathered world
can build a nest
And what magician cast
A magic spell
To make a wonderland
Of wood and dell.

No. Only one, our maker up above
Can recreate our springtime
In wonder and in
Love

Florence Pilkington

ANOTHER DAY

As yesterday's sorrows are fading,
        A light of hope filters through
Bringing with it a new dawn
        Kissed by a fresh morning dew
Life seems a little brighter now
        As the sunshine replaces the rain.
Someone appears on the horizon of hope
        To help ease yesterday's pain
Silently you stand there watching -
        As the river flows into the sea
Knowing that you're not quite ready yet
        To swim in waters of uncertainty
Slowly you walk away from the shore -
        not daring to take the risk
For fear of losing your heart too soon
        from the touch of an innocent kiss
Missed chances bring questions unanswered
        of a memory not to be seen
Regrets will follow with a silent cry
        for a love that may never have been
So take my hand and trust me
        As we live for the day that we see
As yesterday's sorrows are shadows
        Yet today is tomorrow's memory.

Sue Dyson

MY SEASIDE HOME

The Christmas crowds have all gone home
Now January's here
The place looks almost eerie
As I glance along the Pier
Most hotels on the front are shut
There's not a guest in sight
Some owners, if they're lucky
Have booked a sunshine flight
The 'Big one's looming in the sky
The silent fair below
I pass a lone road sweeper
So we nod and say 'Hello'
I must admit I rather like
These two months in each year
When prom and town are quieter
And there's mainly locals here
When March comes round the buzz begins
You feel it in the air
The smell of paint all fresh and new
The things that need repair
The season's in full swing again
The crowds. the shows, the cheer
Pink rock and funny postcards
Saying - 'Wish that you were here'
They're switching on the lights again
The cars queue on the prom
When all this fun is over
That's another year near gone!

Clare Andrews

INFORMATION TECHNOLOGY

Information Technology
So smart and so slick,
Therein problems are
Solved with 'Clickety clicks'
Light emitting diodes
'LEDs' for short,
Computer language
I have brought
To brook . . . as
I've only just slipped
That hook . . . I'm a 'Computer Disputer'
When my culture is downed.
We all have the need
to conquer and share
Not sit like a lion
Alone in his lair.
Books have always been
My friends . . . especially
The ones I didn't
Read in the end
A little knowledge
Is a dangerous thing . . . and
when lights flash and sirens wail
And silicon chips alone prevail
We are all for sale.
ADV For Sale . . .Clickety click

K King

PEACE IN THE LAND OF LOVE

Don't cry for those who are dead and gone
For they're up in Heaven with the Holy one
But pray for the ones who are left behind
Who are going on living with hell on their mind
For every day brings more terrible shocks
Bombs and bullets that never stops
Hatred and shame brought upon this land
This Emerald Isle, this Ireland
Why, oh why must this war go on
This endless rage of their fathers' sons
Upon this green and pleasant land
Which God has made by his loving hand
God is watching as this war goes on
God is listening to the cries of his sons
And maybe someday as they pray for peace
God will say that this war must cease
And we must pray too for this lovely Isle
This Isle with its shamrock and blue blue skies
And we'll all pray to our God up above
To bring peace and hope to this
       Ireland we love.

Joy Murray

THE MOST QUIETEST PLACE

The most quietest place on earth,
There are no noisy neighbours,
No litter or junk to pick up,
No leaky roofs or draughty houses to mend,
The most quietest place is where the living never dwell,
A place of serene tranquillity and calm,
The cemetery.

Reuben Stockwell

SHIRLEY

Gone is the sureness
Directness and caring
Once there was life
Now, slow and stooping

The face that I know
Is changing before me
Where once there was blueness of eye
Now, dullness that's fought
With a courage that shames me

The struggle to speak
To remain as I knew them
Is making me cringe like a dog
A smile through the pain
and the eyes close again

Oh! What a waste
To grow from a sprig to
a tree blooming
Then winter to cover
her face with its blanket

But life is so fleeting
And nature reminds us
In winter as things die away
The spring brings beauty, wonder and glory
Of a beginning again

J Wills

NEXT!

I've summoned up my courage
      And I walk up to the door
But the problem I've been having
      Just isn't there no more

Should I cancel the appointment
      Tell the girl I've got it wrong?
Receptionist - with knowing smile says
      Sit down he won't be long

And so I sit there waiting
      With strangers in a room
Soft music plays and fishes swim
      But this can't dispel the gloom

We fidget with the magazines
      We scarcely read the text
All waiting for the dreaded call
      Of 'So and so in next'

We glance at one another
      And give a smile that's wane
The sudden noise is startling
      Was that a cry of pain?

The one who went before me
      Comes out with shaking knees
'Tis then I hear the dreaded call
      'Next for the dentist please'

Alan Reid

HERON

Hunched like an old man
you scan the shallows with your laser eye.

As drifting shadows ebb and fret
you poise and strike.

And a brief flicker of silver
glints
upon the waiting air.

Stiletto beaked and serpent necked
with sinuous grace you hunch no more.
Then clumsily you climb the breeze
and labour up.

Improbable in flight
you fumble through the awkward sky:
your supple swiftness
sombre-cloaked
awaiting transformation.

Freda Bunce

DISTANT ECHOES

A pendulum swings in regular time
Each tick a year in your distant mind
Some memories old you can't rewind
From childhood days all out of rhyme

From a busy road to a bridle path
From a country lane to a cobbled track
For this is the route of life I walk
Some memories sad wipe off like chalk

124

You must not dwell on times gone by
They are the building blocks of this present guy
To use cement from this present day
To make the bricks of sand and clay

To form a wall of solid stone
Foundations strong like a brand new home
For memories past you want no part
Now is the time for a true fresh start.

Geoffrey Allen

SHADOWS

Shadow of life
Shadow of death
No more pulse
No more breath

Taken to the stars
Lost you in the night
My golden shadow
Put up a brave fight

You were my future
Forced into my past
Emptiness and sorrow
Overwhelm like a black shadow cast

Now I am a shadow of my former self
Become a shadow of life
And a shadow of death
Still with breath

M Houghton

PRIVATE THOUGHTS

The streams within me twist and turn
And overflow sometimes
That's when I think I'm foolish
There is no escape from my mind

But when they run so smoothly
And trickle nicely by
At moments when I pause and sigh
That's when I think I'm wise.

My memory has to register
That quiet place within
It's somewhere in my mind
The one that's hard to find

For when I'm in my quiet place
It's beautiful I know
And lies within us all
Some people call it soul.

Elizabeth Hunter

MY FRIEND

I was so sorry for my friend
She really had it rough
I remember, she once said to me
'I've just had quite enough'

That's how it is with most of us
Sat around with aches and pains
It makes you wish with all your heart
That you were young again.

For when you're young and healthy
Life's just a load of fun
But then the years creep up on you
It's then the troubles come

But we've just got to bear it
And try to wear a smile
And keep on thinking to ourself
That life is still worthwhile.

Ruth Foden

MICE

Oh Barbara, how very nice
To be surrounded by friendly mice,
I'm sure they're tickled pink, that they
On no account can be sent away.
Their little eyes so shiny bright
Can be so scary in the night,
Also their tiny scampering feet
Aren't always what one wants to meet.

I've heard of squatters taking o'er
Someone's house, from roof to floor,
So do give them a cheery greeting
Or they might hold a council meeting
Just to see what's best to do -
Should they vacate the place - or you?

Perhaps it's music that they're after
When they chase around the rafter,
They may like to hear you play
Think you won't send them away,
'Tales of Hoffman' - no, of mice!
I know what I'd do, in a thrice.

J H Heyworth

A-ROVING

Ah 'twas a week of railway fun
So spent with Graham, beloved son.
Rail-roving we went in 87's July,
Routes old and new did we rely.

Nor'-West freedom be ours to share,
Beholding much in sunshine glare!
Miles twentysix hundred we did sped
'Tween sleepers and sleep and appetites fed.

Where we did go embraced the heart,
Though plans did change right from the start;
Oh Windermere we were denied,
Live-wires were down! We could 'ave cried!

Oh how varied did Thursday be
Frae Ribblesdale's Valley and Blackpool's sea;
Yon stream-kissed stones and babies' yell,
Beheld we both, we now do tell.

Clapham's 100 per hour merit their 'spot',
Plus Airway's 'Concorde' to top the lot.
Thus ended our week in eightyseven,
Nationwide next year be our new 'heaven'.

David M Ivey

MORE ASPIRIN PLEASE

He lives between fiction and reality,
This morning sitting in a tub of suds,
Deeper than the night before.

She reclines naked
Eating toast and whisky-marmalade,
Feeding crusts to the birds.

Outside it is very hot,
Too hot to make a hand stir.

In the mirror he sees a mottled sky,
Figurative in stencilled shapes.
He squeezes his aching neck;
And asks for, 'more aspirin please.'

Maureen Weldon

MY WIFE

I often think about my life
And how a friend became my wife
She's always been right by my side
As we travelled life's journey far and wide.

To share our life in sickness and health
Our love together is all our wealth
We made our promises years ago
To love and honour this, I know.

My wife is all my life to me
I only hope that I can see
The sacrifices she has made
The foundations for our love she laid.

And as we reach our middle life
I'm proud to be beside my wife
And as together we grow old
I know our love will not go cold.

And so our life, such love has seen
Together we have always been
To live and love as years go by
This love of ours will never die.

Victor Coulton

THINK OF A SNOWFLAKE

Think of a snowflake, delicate,
drifting, rain crystallised into
white and clustering motion.
Think of the elegant,
intricate forms, the tiny,
six-sided perfection.
Think of the insect flight
from the chasing sky in the
day, six errant spires from
the central church,
six wheels to keep the fall
soft-spinning,
six wings indivisible, steady
firm settings in the unique
pattern soon obliterated by a
snowstorm.

Think of the snowstorm, with
its lilting, unending beauty
now in the night,
its contrast, gentle and
touching, like a torrent of
toppled stars;
then gathering force, collecting
fury, a waterfall of cold
white, lashing silently the
rocks of night.
Gentler again, as a ghost
gliding through the slippery
silver air of a snow world.

Think of the snow world when
the east comes dawning,
when the supply is stemmed
and its roots are slain in
treacherous ground,
when the beeches shiver, their

noble limbs aged in white,
and snow still loping to the
quiet still falls.
When the day is ending, and
meadow grass is patchily
peering through.
Think of the melting, the
salting, the clearance, the
inconvenience, the peril,
the sad excess that was too
generous and gave too much.
Think of the snowflake.

Carolyn F Peck

AULTROY

It is so peaceful here
With trees and hills around
Listening to the wind blowing
Watch snow fall to the ground

I am sitting in a caravan
Very cosy beside the fire
Feeling warm and happy
Dreaming of my heart's desire

This place is very special
I could get used to it here
Not much traffic passing by
As I shed a silent tear

Dreaming of the next time
I go travelling up the west
To all the peace and quiet
The place to get some rest

Jeanette Mackenzie

VOICES

I listen to tiny voices
In the stillness of the night
They tell me little verses
And urge me on to write

Write them down they cry
How excited they become
Until I start to write
Those words in the night

Hurry Hurry they shout
Before the sun comes out
And once I have started
I hear a mighty shout

Sometimes I wonder
Who they really are
Where do they come from
And where do they go

Maybe they are fairies
Pixies or even gnomes
Is that why they know
So many little poems?

I wonder do they live
In a tiny little dell
To dance and to sing
Then to me they bring

Their tiny little verses
So that I can write
In the middle of the night
Before the lark can sing

Then before I have awoke
They vanish in a cloud
Just like a puff of smoke

Ron Dom

TWENTY YEARS

I came to live in Longridge
In nineteen sixty nine
From Cleveleys by the seaside
I thought 'The country's fine'

'Twenty years 'fore tha's one o' us'
The locals said to me
I little knew how right they were
In retrospect I see

I'd greet them with 'Good morning
And how are you today?'
'Aas reet mi owd fine fettler
Is tha?' they used to say

I made a conscious effort
And really tried my best
To become one of the family
Not a cuckoo in the nest

I made mistakes I must admit
As all of us must do
I've also made a lot of friends
And an enemy or two

Life's ups and downs, I've had my share
Widowed twice in just nine years
It's times like this you need good friends
I found them all - right here

I think I've been accepted
My twenty years well gone
'Aas reet an feelin grand as owt'
At last I think I'm one

John Farmery

IMMORTAL

We live to be immortal,
The age-old quest to last,
So we stop ourselves from trying
To avoid what things may pass.
Scared at the foot of future,
That we may lose our feet,
Although we have such feelings
Ourselves we gladly cheat.

For years we've been pretending,
It's like a childish game,
Where pain's the only victor,
Insecurity is to blame.
Despite the past was joyful,
And how the present is,
We continue to avoid it
'Content with all of this.'

All of those around us
Shake heads with deep concern,
And wonder at our folly,
And why we never learn.
Perhaps one day we'll realise
What might, or not, have been,
In hindsight we'll be tortured,
By what we should have seen.

Lini Greenall

HARVEST TIME

There's a greengrocer's shop at the end of our street,
- You know the kind I mean -
With piles of fruit and veg galore,
And herbs tucked in-between.

Throughout the year they do their best
To keep us all supplied
With swedes and onions, carrots too,
And fruit from far and wide.

All summer long we have our pick
Of cherries and strawberries sweet,
There's gooseberries, plums and apricots,
And melons so juicy to eat.

When autumn comes and school begins,
It's harvest-basket time,
With Cox's apples and Williams' pears,
And cabbages in their prime.

It's time to stop and give their thanks,
And we hear young voices sing
Their songs of praise to God on high,
For the gifts of food they bring.

And the greengrocer's shop is a cave of delight,
With reds and russets and gold,
For harvest time is the very best time,
Whether you're young or old.

And when we grow old we can think to ourselves
How we've gained from life's rich store,
And the harvest of wisdom and knowledge we hold
Is ours for evermore.

Hilda Speakman

SWINGS AND ROUNDABOUTS

I'm hooked on watching TV
Almost anything at all,
But switch off all those gameshows
'Cos they drive me up the wall.

I take delight in travel,
Choosing boat, coach, car or bike,
'Cos I hate queues at airports
When Air Traffic go on strike.

I've a weakness for smart men
Who can DIY as well.
I'm turned off by those smoothies
Who have never rung my bell.

I like to get a bargain
When I buy the latest clothes,
But when best friends outdo me,
That sure does get up my nose.

I just adore my husband,
Simply loathe his smelly socks.
He's partial to best bitter,
I prefer Scotch on the rocks.

He revels in the sunshine,
I'm happier in the shade.
But like Jack Spratt and missis
That's how marriages are made.

Roy Gordon

RICH PICKINGS

Cold. So cold.
The flock - silent.
Waiting.
Jittery, glittery eyes
Expectant.

Yellow daggers
demanding survival.

A door slams!
Green boots trudge.
Gloved hand provides.

Feathery bodies collide.
Diving. Pinching. Chasing.

Red bosom bosses
puffed, pompous he
takes his prize.

Blue bonnet antics
on the high-wire amuse.

Feather steals from fur -
Beds and bellies to line.
Rich pickings
till the snow subsides.

Diane Williams

BLACK AND WHITE
(Dedicated to every origin especially 'MF')

Growing together they both knew was wrong,
how could they stop their feelings so strong?
A time for being in another world of peace, not war
that momentous occasion but, only hatred they saw.

Something went wrong during passion with lust
showing no sorrow or guilt through principles of trust.
Expectations, were all gone dictations became lies.
Morals they once believed in are broken but, why?

Maybe cutting their beliefs into small pieces,
they never knew how to iron out those permanent creases
Senior adults took control no-one else could see
their nightmare had started, only a few let it be.

A principle can be slightly scarred but, never torn.
Those threats upon two people are but left to mourn.
Disapproval, disappointment gone for them never to return.
Still together now surely a statement to learn.

Julie Keel

CHANGE OF SCENE

We've been away, just briefly,
Enjoyed a change of scene,
Walked on sandy shores,
Climbed rocky paths,
Explored valleys lush and green.
Espied sweet violets at the wayside,
Watched the sheep with lambs in tow,
Collected shells and pebbles with our faces all aglow.

The time went by so quickly,
Soon we had to journey back
With lots of happy memories, stored up and kept intact.
Yet - when familiar landmarks claim the view
I always thrill with pride, anew,
How true it is where e'er you roam
There really is no place like home!

Nancy J Owen

THE NEW HOUSE

The sales office staff have conned us again
They promised completion they promised us men
To sort out the problems and finish the house
But nothing is ready and so I must grouse

The windows are dirty and so is the floor
The curtains aren't here and they've jammed the French door
The loft light is missing and so are the phones
They say there's no problem ignoring our groans

A week I've been trying to sort out the money
The sales office attitude really ain't funny
I thought for a while it would all end in tears
Allegedly they have been like this for years

Now we are in tho' it was a bit tricky
They were laying new road making everything sticky
The family is sleeping exhausted by panic
The dog is exploring and acting quite manic

But this is our home for better or worse
To some it's a blessing to many a curse
To us it's commitment we've chosen to share it
Whatever the future together we'll bear it

Tony Hatton

LOST LOVE

Memories treasured from long ago
Still remain - is that not so?
I loved you so much
I could not let go

Sad though it seems - drifting apart
The cut is so deep - inside my heart
Wounds always heal
A part of me still feels

I could not have given more
To someone I loved
Maybe I was wrong
You are the one
Who will always be strong

V A Tunstall

THE DANDELION DAME

The Dandelion Dame,
For that is her name,
Is common, raucous and loud.

Unwanted, still claims
To spread yellow flames,
By abundance in seed
And abundance in greed.

Tenacious in strength
By her long root length:
Though brazen and crude
Is remarkably successful!

Heather Bolton

GONE FISHING

I'm not too keen on tennis
Or going for a run
'Cos fishing is my hobby
It's my idea of fun

The type of fish I catch
Are always very large
They're perfect when they're fried
With a little bit of marge!

I never catch mere tiddlers
I'm far too good for that
Though some friends have accused me
Of talking through my hat!

I'm fond of my dear maggots
My tackle's my best friend
My hobby's very soothing
When I'm going round the bend

Fishing is very fitting
For someone of my age
I'm totally convinced
That I'm past the jogging stage

So if you've never tried it
Don't mock the fisherman
Just try standing with your rod
And you'll soon become a fan!

A Goodrum

MY CANDLE WAX IS HOT

Light flickers - the wind blows
And I am dark.
Unknown with only me and the night
For company.
I hate love - love hate and the
Colour is
      Gone
            My eyes are blind
To people; to him. And I am and the sky is
Blue. With clouds of grey and the sun's rays black.
      The thorns are still
Sharp. In my heart and in my mind
I see a flame. On my fingers I feel
Sadness. Blood is red, tears are wet and
So is my memory.
      I can do
            Better - than who?
              Or what?
             I do care and
          The candle wax is always hot.

Lindsay Gale

EVERY DAY AND NIGHT

Every single night, I say that same old prayer,
Hoping that some day, he will really care.
I want him to hear me.
I want him here with me.

But in his world, I am not included,
Yet anything he does, I am not deluded.
He'll never see
The feelings inside me.

Every single day, I get that same old feeling,
As though something about him is going to be revealing.
My hopes begin to rise
When he looks into my eyes.

But these hopes that I have will never come true.
He will never say, 'I love you.'
Dreams will not deceive me,
So why don't I believe me?

Laura McAulay

WHITE DEATH

First you hear a thunderous roar
Next a panic, screams and more
Grab your essentials, take your fear
Don't hang around to collect your gear
It's so powerful, it's so much stronger
It's hard to believe, how much longer?
Don't slow down, for a last glance
Don't be selfish, give them a chance
Someone's last in every queue
Who's at the back? It could be you!
Find a safe distance, away from the dangers
Escape with your life, with hundreds of strangers
Hearing again, still clear is the sound
Wondering if it's your doors, it has found
Now a refugee and your losses are high
It's not just material things, you don't sleep, you just lie
Time passes slowly, but the climate is bitten
We realise our biographies, must be re-written
Walking back home, with your neighbour's hand
Seeing for the first time, the substitute land

Lisa McCrakan

THE LEOPARD

When the leopard has gone
And the great muddied prints fill my house,
The furniture torn and made irrelevant
The doors aswing, the house itself
Become a poor shell mimicry of jungle,
What next?
How impossible to reinvent belief in walls and roof,
Neighbours and helpful living,
How build a house again
Where leopards do not come?
Yet why step out onto that muddied path,
Emptier still,
Where all the heaving green
Echoes to the absence of those
Unreturning savage calls?

Helen Armstrong

MY LETTERS

At my desk I like to sit and write
Always in the late of night,
Pen-pal letters all in place
In a pile by my pencil case,
Telling them about the weather
And the things the family have done together,
They tell me what they think and say -
I love receiving letters every day
Each one gives me so much pleasure,
I think of them all as my little treasures!

Blanche Farley

THE HOUSE BY THE SEA

An attic in a house with a sea view,
In Cleveleys, the holiday home my brother and I knew,
The sand from the shore came up to the door,
Nana always paid 'cos Mother and Daddy were poor.

We came in a hired car, not common those days,
I am going back not to the 1930's ways,
We were content to play with the shells in the sand
My brother and I, happy hand in hand.

From the attic window we'd watch a little boat sail,
If that old boatman were here he'd tell a good tale,
Like the day he took us out for a sixpenny trip,
He drifted too far, and made us all sick.

The only circus there was in town,
Was six white poodles, and a what-is-it horse clown,
There was Tommy who gave an open-air show,
He had us all on his stage to gave a 'go'

Then that coin machine on Victoria Road,
You'd almost to fill it before out came a load,
We spent our shilling pocket money on buying pink rock,
And a delicious sweet called 'Eular' in a dainty box.

Now I live in Cleveleys, and I walk to the shore,
Everything's changed, yet my memories I store,
Because left of that family, there's now only me,
Though the attic's there, in that house by the sea.

Margaret Openshaw

MONEY MAIL

I heard the postman's ratta-ta-tat.
I picked up my mail dropped on the mat
I know that there will surely be
A fortune to be won - just you see
Open this envelope without delay
This could be your lucky day
If your personal number it does tally
Well; there you are you have a chance of holiday in Bali
And when the little flap you are told to lift
Well, there you see - you've won a free gift
They are not kidding it really is true
Post this now - before the closing date's due
One man in your area - not very far
Was delighted to hear he'd won a car.
Just scratch off three numbers you cannot lose
There you are, see, you're in a draw for a cruise
And then there's the offer of saving cash
But put on your skates - the prize - a Trolley Dash
And so with all these offers that come in the mail
The dream of a fortune cannot fail
But I know in my heart I'll never win
As soon as I've read them they go straight in the bin

Kathleen Plummer

SECRET LANCASHIRE

Dirty mills, grubby streets
Back to back houses and clog-shod feet.
Pit head and slag heap,
Smoke and grime,
Lowery and Greenwood in their prime.

Fell top and heather, grouse on the wing,
This is a vision to make the heart sing.
No sign of chimney stacks. No dirty terraces
But farmyards and cottages
This is our heritage.

M Taylor

MOT - MINE OR THERES

How come when a car breaks down
it is easy enough to call someone out
to tow it away, to get it repaired in
a couple of days.
Cars are fixed and put back on the
road no matter what the costs.
Most people have their cars insured
so they are covered for their debts,
but man himself has some kind of
a breakdown, but has to join the
queue, to wait for operations for
repairs or to see someone for medications
to take.
None of us have spare parts so we
wait for spare parts of someone else,
who has passed away and outlived their
stay, but their organs will be transferred
to live yet another day and help
someone else prolong their stay.

Patricia McDonough

THE OLD DERELICT HOUSE

sweet sex by the riverside.
I remember when we would run and hide.
The others searching, in the shadows we'd lie.
Now I'm counting the years gone by.

Recall the old derelict house.
In the day only been there twice.
But later on, French kisses in the darkened doorway.
Well it got late, they went away, but we chose to stay.

Tracks rumble train passes in the night.
Look fast and you can see the cabin lights.
After nights of play our clothes were dirty and our clothes were torn.
And your hands were so cold but your lips were warm.

I can still see her in the field where we used to go.
I can still feel her in the places where we'd lie low.
And when I walk along the river and the railway line.
I can still hear her whisper.

>   Let's go to the old derelict house.
>   In the day only been there twice.

Adam Griffiths

CHILD OF CONFLICT . . .

Gone is the child you briefly glimpsed
gone too the wooden sword and bow
aware is he that flesh can tear that bullets
kill that blood will flow

With rusted spikes and barbed wire maze
a distant sounding drum . . behold the child of
innocence . . a hooded man with gun

Christopher McKeever

148

MY TWO FACES

The mirror hanging on the wall
Never tells me any lies
What I see, is what I am
With wrinkles round my eyes,

I used to see a young man
Spruce, and up-to-date
Now I see an older man
With a slightly balding pate,

As each day passes by
I can see more of me
A little here, a little there
And I don't like what I see,

But I don't feel an old man
I never have in fact
So I close my eyes and imagine
That I'm not as old as that,

But deep down inside of me
I know that it is not so
For me to think I'm twenty-one
When I'm seventy seven you know,

Well there is no harm in thinking
That the image that I see
Is not the older person I know I am
But the younger one I'd like to be.

Charles O Desjarlais

UNREQUITED LOVE

The great poets write of unrequited love
And that is all I can ever think of
I need your affection, your thoughts and your touch
But could I be simply asking too much?
I long to be in your company
But you never seem to notice me
I yearn to touch your silken skin
But I know that you won't let me in
The things I say don't ever sound right
But I can't tell the truth - I don't want us to fight
Without you I'll never be satisfied
And I can't understand all those times when I lied
To get out of things that were so hard to say
But if I'd said them, would you have cared anyway?
When you're talking to me, I just can't handle it
I hope and wish it was more than it is
But everything you do is simply a game
My heart skips a beat when I hear your name
Your nonchalant air leaves me in awe
The shape of your neck, the line of your jaw
Flip your hair, adjust your hands
My devotion, I cannot understand
I try to pretend that it's not true
That I'm hopelessly in love with you
You are my one and only ambition
Please give me your recognition
I'd do anything for you, whatever you asked
Nothing would ever be too hard a task
Falling in love can be painful, it's true
I'm falling, I'm falling, I'm falling for you.

Zoë Caine

GOODNIGHT MR MOON

The crystal gaze
Of your friendly face
Was a comfort in my room
You calmed my fears and
Secret tears

So goodnight Mr Moon

Could you feel my hurt
Above the earth
As you sailed across the sky?
A thousand prayers of love
And care
Must have passed before
Your eyes.

And you say a shining angel
Will guide me on my way,
Lighting the night with love
That's bright
Though tears I fear plead stay.

But you know I must be leaving
I should not linger on life's stage
Beyond the stars to wander
Free at last from pain.

So goodnight Mr Moon

I'm glad to have said hello
The comfort which you gave me
Glowed about my home,
But do not dwell in sadness
There's peace beyond the sky,
Gentle wings to silently bear us
Until we reach the other side.

Phillip Moore

IF ONLY

If only I was grown up, I'd make sure all of nature
Was looked after, the forests would never go away.

If only I was the sun, I'd shine down with all my might
At the dawn of each new day.

If only I was a tree, I'd be an old, wise oak,
Everyone would listen to what I had to say.

If only I was a field of wheat, I'd sway gently in the breeze,
Protecting all life that lived within my hay.

If only I was a bull, I'd stand in my field looking
Fearsome and grand, daring people to come and play.

If only I was a flower, I'd open my coloured petals
Towards the sun, drinking in every golden ray.

If only I was a field mouse, I'd scamper about
With my friends, we'd all be happy and gay.

If only I was a butterfly, I'd show off my patterned wings
To every passer-by, on the scented lilac bush I'd lay.

If only I was a spider, I'd spin shining webs of silk
Amongst the hedgerows without delay.

If only I was a bee, I'd buzz from flower to flower
Collecting pollen in early May.

If only I was a horse, I'd canter around the country,
Tossing my long, chestnut mane with a neigh.

If only I was an owl, I'd watch out for all night-time
Creatures keeping evil at bay.

If only I was the moon, I'd throw out enchanting silver
Light upon night-time travellers, guiding their way.

If only I was a child, I'd still see things this way,
But I'm all grown up now, I'm twelve today.

K & J Halliwell

FINAL DAYS ARE HERE

Casting shadows on the ground
Leaves brush past me standing still
Of stained glass windows painted black
Of candles on my window sill
No noise, no people just dark skies
Of restless armies on they fight
Hunts man's dogs with bated breath
And in the day the cold of night
Of paper blowing round a tree root
Of oceans lapping against no beach
Of one man lying on the ground
Still preachers bold begin to preach
Of air that stings to breath again
To stay indoors to hide the sun
To walk to laugh all a crime
And children hide or else they run.
And metallic the gleam a stranger beast
To take away the rest we hope
As planes fly over in past days
The fishermen with still no rope
The bible falls open onto the floor
And the ground begins to shake
To take each life all at once
The earth to rot the sky to break.

Heather Martyn

DAD

I remember the man who was my dad,
A carpenter by trade,
In memory, carved and fashioned
Like the childhood toys he made.

He was a loving, caring father,
Mindful of a daughter's needs
And although no longer with me,
I recall each word and deed.

The happy times we spent together
Can never be replaced,
And the memory of him serves me well
As life's parade I taste.

Valerie A Cottier

LUNCHTIME IN THE PARK

Alone I sit on a bench in the park,
Watching the world go by. Around the swings,
Slide, and see-saw, roundabout, and things
Like climbing frames, children play, and dogs bark.
Beyond this activity, a man sat on
A bench is joined by another. A pair
Of souls may have so many things to share;
Could have so many secrets in common.
Yet they hardly look at one another,
Let alone speak: embarrassed to be there,
Side by side, minding their own business.
Or maybe, perhaps, they couldn't care less
About each other. Surely, I should be
More sociable than the man sat next to me?

Chris Moores

UNTITLED

Ah, those times
How we forgot to think
Nothingness found us
The missing link
Ability used in the idle abyss
Where we're free to roam
Without being missed
Days and nights
Middle and end
Are different this way to comprehend

Lloyd Sonnier

HIDDEN PAST

The dawning sapphire sky I see
When the stars at night show me my destiny
May the stars guide sailors this lowly, dark night
In the sapphire sky I'll watch the eagle take to flight
My past's too far gone it's travelled out of sight
I need a real friend to tell me it's all right.

Tell me it's all right to forget the past
Or am I taking this all too fast?
I am like an eagle, I fly away from my fears
But my past catches up, it all ends in tears
Tell me it's all right to confess all to you
I'll be a shoulder for you to cry on too

Tell me it's all right to believe what I believe
To never let my heart to darkness conceive
I am like the sailors, I miss people I leave behind
The stars are a small comfort, but as compass they're signed
Tell me it's all right for this sadness to end
I know you'll always be there with a hand to lend.

Caroline Sweeney

THE ROBIN

Friendly robin
Always bobbin'
Utter your merry song.

Worms search,
Alert perch,
The gardener comes along.

Insects catch,
Seeds despatch,
Ingenious little bird.

Rotund creature
National feature,
Silvery cadence heard.

Flowerpot nest,
Red breast,
Standing near the holly.

White tummy,
Yummy, yummy,
Grubs are very jolly.

Sharp eye,
Berries spy,
Peck them with your beak.

Red throat,
Brown coat,
Friendship with us seek.

Eleanor Dalton

THE SEEKER OF SOULS

Please don't turn the light out Mummy . . .
the little child said,
as he heaved his weary little body,
into his daunting bed.
'Now don't be silly Tommy, I'll see you in the morning'
said the shadow of his mother
in between the yawning.

Tommy crept between the covers,
hoping there not be . . .
something, hiding, waiting, lurking,
someone he'd not seen!
He slowly dazed into a dream, oblivious
to the fact,
that in the shadows something lurked . . .
with whom the devil made a pact.

Its rasping breath he did not hear,
its icy touch not feel,
as it slipped into the darkness, with the
likeness of an eel . . .
At the gates of Satan, a knocking did commence . . .
'Who's there?' uttered the doorman,
'The Seeker of Souls . . . '
it said.

As Mother rose she shuddered, but knew not
what for or why . . .
and in the silence of his room rang
Tommy's pleading cry.

Please don't turn the light out Mummy . . .

Nicola Tombs (15)

DRIFTING IN SPACE

I feel like a spacemen, lost in the stars
I've turned into a prisoner, locked behind bars
I'm searching for a reason to end this sorry state
But all you can do in prison is sit and wait.

I wish I had the answers, I wish it was so clear
So I could see myself, begin to reappear
You're all so blind, you can't see how trapped I am
Half of you don't know me, half of you don't give a damn
But, if I could climb out of his clutches away from this hell
You'd notice the difference, you'd be able to tell.

I feel like a radio station, tuned to the wrong frequency
Everyone's out there, but no-one can hear me
A voice that speaks with its mind, not his lips
Like a cinema that won't show a film, just the clips
I'm killing myself and there's nothing I can do
He's stuck inside me, he's stuck like glue
Fighting with myself, losing valuable time
I'm sick of pretending everything's fine
I don't want you thinking this is who I be,
I am the person, locked inside me
But for me to escape, and start playing the game
I have to become senseless, to deal with the pain
Ignore all those feelings in the back of my mind
Ignore all those voices that made me go blind.

James O'Donovan

158

SILVER TONGUE

I can't look you in the eye
when my own skulk in shadows,
disappointing children at the zoo.
But when you've passed
I come out and beg for food.

I can't open the door to a pub,
but I'll slip into a friend's shadow.
A sociable wave crashes over my head;
I can't swim ! I can't swim!
Though I'll cling to the shore like a crab.

I can't tell you what I think,
but I'll nod and grunt
while my opinions form into ice-cubes
behind gritted teeth,
though my lines are rehearsed to a fault.

I won't take centre stage
but now it's too late,
for I can see the head of this poem.
There is no silver tongue,
but its eyes meet mine.

Marc Lines

PROFESSIONAL CONDUCT

Katherine, a devoted Alternative,
For her practitioner grew yearnative,
The professional homeopath
Said 'I can't be your Romeo Kath,
Etiquette requires I be spurnative.'

Ann Banks

TIME IS SO PRECIOUS

Let me tell you once more that I love you
For one day it may be too late
For time passes by so quickly
It could be taken from me by fate.

Let me offer you a life's devotion
And whisper so true
That I'll treasure forever
The great love I have for you.
And because time goes by so quickly
For day soon turns to night
I'll keep on telling you
Until time stops its endless flight.

Let me thank you for being so caring
And for a truly wonderful life
For I've made the most of my time
As your very devoted wife.

J M Gilchrist

PAINTING CONSTELLATIONS

Star fields burning.
Blue and white,
Sizzle spots on indigo . . . psssss . . .
. . . ssss - swillowing matter pen.
Starts up there, comes down here,
Ether to paper.
Picture forming, letters curving,
Routeing wordy shapes,
Cod.

Colin Jacklin

THIS FREEDOM

We came home,
glad that it was over
the tyranny defeated and all the peoples free.

We saw the snuffed out ruins
and the wasteland,
the shattered lives of those
left alone
and hoped that
it was worth it.

We did not count the cost,
not then,
it was too great.
But we knew the price we'd paid for freedom,
it was written on the graves.

And now we who are left are old
and peer through our glasses
at this new world
we do not understand.
This free world,
too free for us who made it so.

This brave new world,
with new names for old sins.
Ethnic cleansing, the new genocide,
terrorism, the cowards' war.

So hard to take
this shattering of our dreams,
the betrayal of the youthful dead.
An unsafe world without control,
A licence that is freedom's child,
Is that what we won?

Arthur Denny

ACQUAINTANCE

If the world were just
A dark hole of hatred
You'd be my light
So bright and sacred.
If the world were just
A vast, open desert
You'd be my oasis
In the hot sticky weather.
How could you know
You mean so much to me
When through my mind
You cannot see?
All I can do is
Write this for you
And hope you feel
The same way too.
So whenever you feel
Life just isn't fair
Even if we're not talking,
I'll always be there.

Wanawsha Baban (17)

LOVE

As years go by and time does pass
Remember the day we sat on the grass
We kissed each other and cuddled so tight
Cupid was hovering around us that night
We gazed at the stars in the sky up above
We looked at each other we were falling in love
Our hearts were racing with a burning desire
Nothing on earth could put out this fire.

We are a couple who love one another
We laugh and giggle like sister and brother
Nothing can break us we are like a heart
We beat together and don't fall apart
Love is a feeling we all own and possess
It brings to us all joy and happiness
Time is ticking away each day
Love is forever and will always stay.

Mary Kirby

GENESIS?

Cast aside your earthly guise,
Evacuate your mind,
Climb up to a higher place
And gaze down on mankind.

Look and see what man can do,
Unto his fellow man,
And wonder how he came on earth,
How come it all began?

The Bible says he came from God
With Adam in the lead,
And all the nations of the world
Developed from his seed.

But science tells a diff'rent tale,
About humanity,
It says he came from creatures
That came crawling from the sea.

And now you've seen what man can do
What will your answer be,
Did he come from God above
Or from the slimy sea?

Robert A Bland

OUR DAY

(This was the day! Entirely ours!
Stolen from Time and Eternity!)
Climbing the height
In rapt delight
Our souls took flight
Into a rapturous destiny . . .

We were one with the wind,
The cold - wild - wind -
Which blew all around us -
And through us and o'er us.
Which bathed us and blessed us,
Which kissed and caressed us,
       Baptised us with ice
       And re-bore us with fire!

We were one with the hills . . .
The proud free hills . . .
Which curved all around us
And witnessed our vows.

We were one with the trees -
Their beauty was ours,
Their strength and their grace
And their wild singing bowers.

What of the sky? The glorious sky -
That wonder, which dazzled us,
Dazed us, o'erwhelmed us
Enthralled us and bound us
In rapturous awe!

This was the day, the day that was ours!
All glory and goodness,
All joy and delight!
All beauty and loveliness,
All radiance all happiness.
Too quickly, oh day you were one with the night!

Nora Smith

UNTITLED

Sometimes, when we sleep apart
together within our own domain,
is separate dreams we share
a mutual aim, or so it seems.

And sometimes in nocturnal trance
you turn to me with restless limbs,
that speak no language but you chance;
refused advances. You rescind

as morning searches out your flesh;
that skin you wear so well,
between the starched-white linen sheets
where dormant passions dwell.

Into chaos where the Devil meets
your pound of conditional flesh
and the mercy of the morning greets
with sunlight on naked distress.

And swimming in pools of morning light
float upon your final breath,
before you drown beneath your starched-white sheets
and sink slowly to your death.

John William Hardy

STARS IN THE NIGHT SKY

Take my words into your mind
And let it view the care and kind,
To see not you are blind.
Do you not feel the power
As you read within this sacred hour?
If you feel not, do not fear
Take my hand for I am near,
By your side, within your thoughts
Without each other we are naught
Hopes that shine in our eyes
Flicker as stars in the night sky.

I often walk alone
And hear the distant moan.
Tormented souls without hope
Frantic in the dark they grope
So pained but oh, they try
They hurt so yet still get by,
Piercing wails, how they cry!
Please tell me how to help
And quell their pitiful yelp
Please tell me from the screams
Will they rise into their dreams?
Are hopes that shine in our eyes
As distant as stars in the night sky?

Graham Elleray

MISSING

Soft winds flutter through the pale green leaves,
Fields are stacked with rows of golden sheaves,
Poppies dance upon the trembling breeze,
But you aren't there.

White clouds float across the deep blue skies,
Circling curlews call their plaintive cries,
Silent teardrops fall from sad, dark eyes,
But you aren't there.

Dark moors in their ever changing mood,
Paths where only grazing sheep intrude,
Call me in their lonely solitude,
But you aren't there.

White-capped waves on a deserted shore,
Granite cliffs from which the seagulls soar,
Places you and I used to adore,
But you aren't there.

Noise and traffic in the city street,
Smiling faces as young lovers meet,
Memories which are all so bittersweet,
But you aren't there.

Quiet churchyard on a lonely hill,
No bird sings and all the world is still,
A grave on which my tears forever spill,
For you are there.

Joyce Beardsworth

RAINBOW CITY

(Written for a Song for Salford Competition)

Walter Greenwood in his autobiography
Said there was a time when people lived in poverty
Love was on the dole and the streets were black as coal
People sang for food and money and there was no taste of honey
  Salford City, you are known as a dirty old town
  In the old poverty that has gone I have no pity
  But I have lived here for many a year
  Yet I still spare a tear for scenes that have gone.

Terraces back to back are no more
High-rises take over the city floor
People living high on high
Rising into the dank dark sky
Cut off from all they have known
Now sitting all alone
Salford City, is this your future?
Or will you bring your people down to earth
Where they can talk and socialise
Care and laughter no longer to despise
Like the best of yesterday.
  Salford City, you are known as a dirty old town
  In the old poverty that has gone I have no pity
  But I have lived here for many a year
  Yet I still spare a tear for scenes that have gone.

Philip John Loudon

TREES

I love to stand and look at trees,
Their branches wafted by the breeze.
In winter, without their leaves, so bare,
But sill hiding the birds who nested there.
Sometimes, the branches are heavy with snow,
And sometimes, kissed by frost you know.
But when the winter is gone, and away cold winds,
Spring enters the world, and with her brings
A few showers and the welcome sun,
And watching the trees, we see life has begun.
For the leaf buds appear, so tiny on each bough,
But they grow quickly, making the tree majestic now.
The birds they flutter in and out,
Into their nests and round and about.
Summer arrives, and stays with us a while,
And as she leaves, and takes her smile,
Autumn comes close, turning leaves russet hue,
And some of the birds look for homes anew.
A few will stay, and huddle close as can be,
For the only home they know is the tree.
The leaves gently falling now on the ground,
Serve to remind us that winter comes around
Bringing again the frost, and the snow,
But throughout the seasons trees still grow,
And I am pleasured by them all the year,
And by trees, I love to be near.

J Ahmadi

THE CHIMNEY SWEEP

T he soot was black.
H e put it in his sack.
E very chimney he would climb.

C himneys full of black grime.
H ouses big, houses small,

I nside chimneys short and tall.
M oving up the chimney stack

N o light at all. It was very black.
E ver closer to the sky

'Y es I have done it,' he would cry.

S oot on your skin, and in your hair
W ash, wash, it's everywhere.

E at your supper, little sweep
E yes are tired, it's time to sleep.

P illow soft like ice-cream.
        Go to sleep it's time to dream.

Laura Hoyland (10)

LANCASHIRE A BEAUTY SPOT

You might think Lancashire is a dump but
Don't believe what you hear,
Come up for a holiday and have a look,
At the hills the fields and dry stone walls.
You will not believe your eyes,
There is history and beauty all about.
The only thing you have to do is. Come up
And have a look.

Donald Jay

GOD'S SON ON EARTH

What could he do to prove his worth?
This Sacred Man who was sent to earth to try to save our souls.
As humbly, the Blessed Land he trod
Immortal being, Son of God
(His) Love - A light to show the way
and lead us to a perfect day.

Faith never failing, good and kind
(He) raised the dead
Gave sight to the blind.
But could not open the eyes of those *who would not see.*
Such miserable, wretched people they would be.

We marvel at his words divine
Turning water, at a wedding, into wine.
A tired and hungry multitude were fed
on two small fish, and just five loaves of bread.

(His) disciples he carefully chose, they stayed beside him night and day.
Often they would feel despair, but would never cease to kneel and pray.
He was tempted by the evil tongue of *he*
who perpetuated wrong.

With Godly strength he suffered the strife which came upon him
throughout his life.
At the end, he sat amongst his chosen few
and said, 'A promise I do ask of you, that every year you will come
together, and remember the hours which we spent together, a glass of
wine, break some bread, I'm weary now, I must rest my head.'

Condemned to death upon a stake
'Our Lord' had one last request to make.
'Forgive them for they know not why,
For them I shall live, for them I die.'

V Clegg

WRITE ALTERNATIVE

'It's good to talk,' Bob Hoskins said.
His chatter leaves me cold.
It's good? He talks to earn his bread.
That's how he gets his gold.

But silence is a golden thing.
It doesn't cost so much
As phone calls with a pricey sting.
'It's nice to keep in touch.'

But how can phoney things be great
That interrupt and pressure,
Hassle us, while letters wait
Politely on our pleasure?

When letters that can be re-read
Come smiling through the post
It's true when all is done and said
Nice letters please us most.

Letters don't intrude, they wait
For us to read at leisure.
Take your pen to celebrate.
Write! Letters we can treasure.

Cecil Beach

SWEET ANGELIC CLAIRE

She mirrors the sun,
A morning bright and fair,
She mirrors the beauty
we poets look upon,
the smile
of sweet angelic Claire . . .

Gerald Aldred Judge

THE BLESSINGS OF THE MANX

We who live on the Isle of Man
give thanks to God, where 'ere we can,
For its hills and beaches, beauty too -
with every corner giving a different view.
We've peace, tranquillity, food to eat
folk to talk to, friends to meet.

How different from some other places
where fighting occurs, 'tween feuding races,
Famine and pestilence are their lot
their homes are burnt, there crops do rot.
There is no trust, no-one's a friend
no wonder they ask 'Will it never end?'

Then count we our blessings, one and all
so that into debt, we may not fall,
Why do we have as much as this?
While others in their lives do miss
What we for granted take - and then
forget the sufferings of our fellow men.

We look around this glorious isle
and give our thanks with happy smile.
Here such things happened, long ago
when Vikings were our dreaded foe.
May all have peace, food, beauty we enjoy
every living human, woman, man, girl and boy.

Brian Humphreys

LAMENT

The strength of my weakness,
It must be over at last,
The total dismay forms a shroud,
Of suffocating shattered glass,
The pain is too much to bear,
But I can't feel a thing.
I abused the sentiment,
And locked away existence itself,
Now yesterday rings in my ears,
Abstracting the view of tomorrow.
Negativity screams through the air,
Tearing warm flesh from the bone,
Darkening the already tinted life I saw.
Once I held the melting sky,
But the flames grew high and I just watched it burn,
All reason suppressed by riots of indecision.
The sun will rise again,
Yet my thirst for sleep is satisfied.

Rachel Mandale (17)

HOMETOWN

I thought I knew these streets
These pavements under my feet
I thought I knew each corner
Each nook and cranny of the plan

But this town has
Become a strange town
And though I thought
I'd been around
I am lost in my hometown

I thought I knew the way
Where my dreams could have their day
I thought I was in the middle
But I am on the outside

For this town has
Become a strange town
And though I thought
I'd been around
I am lost in my hometown.

Ian Barton

VAGUE

distinguish acceptable
defined by a dream of beyond
what is right
when thrown into life was not our birth made plea
air hung heavy pink and misted
inside the chamber rules were made
to be discussed
separated maybe even adhered to.

freedom, flowers, dust not daydreams
memories, midblue sky,
nerves shed
shoes tread the unforgotten paths.
forks pierced fruits.
rusty links in the system
sad when expectations go
society faked the must
but new
renew and it all looks clear
stormy nights return to calm.

Janis Robinson

QUESTION

I'm sometimes asked the question.
What it is I see,
Gazing at a landscape
Or looking out to sea.
Standing in a certain place,
Clearing my mind.
Even seeing ugly things,
A kind of beauty find.
Just how, I can't explain this
If they cannot see.
The beauty in creation,
A blade of grass, a tree.
The turmoil of a stormy sea
As winds fragment on high,
The heavy laden storm clouds
Covering the sky.
Reflections in a stagnant pool
Shattered by the rain,
And as the shower goes on by
Reflections see again.
All these things are beautiful,
At least they are to me.
Did God make all this beauty
Just for me to see?

Fred Kenrick

POEM ON POEM

A poem, so they say,
Is like a rare and precious gem
That we handle, and we treasure
Time and time again.

Looking into its beauty;
Deep inside its core.
Should we handle it with reverence,
Should we handle it with awe?

Or should we see
What pleases me
And not what someone says should be?

Is it puzzle? Is it pearl?
Does it matter what it means;
If it's plain as paper,
Or as pretty as it seems?

If it's sad, or funny,
If it rattles round your brain?
It's only pattern playtime
With crystal words again.

So see that inner beauty
Sparkle as we turn
A phrase, or two,
It's up to you;

Maybe then we'll enter
That molten crystal centre
And breathe . . .
For a moment . . .
The fires of the earth.

Debbie Houghton

STAN, I LOVE YOU

Stan, I love you
Guess you know that by now.
I couldn't live without you,
but I wouldn't want to anyhow.

We have our ups
and we have our downs,
Yet you make me smile
admidst the frowns.

We don't need no others
we're better left alone.
As long as we have each other
we're happiest in our home.

We have something between us
that no-one else can touch.
A bond of love that binds us
united by our trust.

You're more precious than silver
much rarer than gold,
Your love I shall cherish
until I grow old!

Pauline Johnston

GOD IS

God is a crack of lightning in a storm,
God is the goodness in an ear of corn,
God is truth from all life came,
God is God since this world began.
God is a tree, his branches spreading,
God is a crisis in a newspaper heading.

God is good, our troubles mending,
God is love, love without ending.
God is God and ever shall be,
If God is good, then God help me.

Barbara Kiernan

YOUR FRIEND AND MINE

Have you ever met my Friend?
You'll know Him if you do.
He'll stay with you right to the end,
He'll show His love is true.
He comes with many faces,
He plays a leading part -
you'll find Him in all places,
right now He's in my heart.

Any promise He will keep,
He'll be always at your call.
My Friend never seems to sleep
He watches over all.
When you're sad and feeling low -
really down and blue,
call for my Friend, and He will show,
to prove His love for you.

Although your eyes may not perceive
and you think no-one is there,
you'll meet my Friend if you believe
and He'll take you in His care.
Then feel honoured just to be
taken by my Friend,
to walk together, you and He,
until the journey's end.

Ron Sherrington

COMICAL KEN

Having first heard the news concerning Ken Dodd -
I could only assume that he'd gone all mod.
He's our toothy comedian - from Knotty Ash -
Seems he's been keen to keep all of his cash -evading the revenue -
And refusing to pay his tax - how could he be so stolidly lax?
It's odd of Dodd to step out of line - he's been comically artistic
                                    since the age of nine -
Working so hard and doing just fine.
It's all so absurd - not unlike others. I can hardly believe one single world -
Yet supposedly he's guilty - as the majority appear to fear -
It'll be a shattering blow to his lifestyle as well as his stage career.
If he leaves those diddy men behind - they'll be lonesome - and that's unkind
The Jam Butty Mines might grind to a halt. And that would also be his fault.
His tickling stick deserves a special mention -
It's a dazzling gimmick of his own invention to bring his fans to pay attention
'Happiness' is his favourite song hit - we love every bit of it -
We're - all of us here - quite fond of Ken. He's much nicer
                                    than Eastenders Den -
We're hopeful that he'll soon recover from all his cares of woe -
So that he'll continue to warmly entertain us all on 'The Ken Dodd Show'.

Eleanor Haydon Sanderson

MANKIND'S FATE

Tower the machines of moon-blue metal
Over our heads of dull inertia;
Shining and strong and in faultless fettle
Fling faded flowers on the tomb of mankind.
In his inventions, the pride of his heydays,
Lay the intrinsic fate of Man;
Gone is the lure of industry's pay days,
Smothered in weeds is the broken dam.

W E M Phillips

180

A THOUGHT
CROSSED MY MIND

If I descend to those depths
I am lost in ruthless ambition
embroiled in a conspiratorial career
a complete politician;
forsaken by good men
holding principle dear,
who would now and then
listen . . .
but that is all.

John Ledgerton

SUN ON A SUNDAY

The giant yellow headed daisies sway in the gentle breeze,
Bowing their heads to approve the hovering bees partaking -
Of the abundance of pollen suspended amongst the petals.

As the sun rests behind a plumped up cushion of white fluffiness -
The sunbather, opens one eye and risks a peek at the sky,
Lazily gazing up at a bird on high, so high, its kind is indefinable.

An outstretched hand reaches and grasps the tall cool glass with straw -
Put to lips that part as easily as a baby's would at the breast.
With sudden eruption the searing sun re-appears.

The sunbather squints and adjusts the brightly coloured sunshade,
Reclining now, then listening to the whirring of a distant lawnmower -
Contrasting against the jingle of an anonymous radio station.

Breathing deeply, the scent of coconut oil wafts up to her nostrils,
Raising the glass in salute of the moment, she whispers 'Thank heaven for -
Sun on a Sunday,' and drifts away again to forget about Monday.

Jan McLean

REAP THE WILD HARVEST

And now the harvest we reap
of those seeds sown during that last Great War,
when the unwelcome stink of death,
third partner in many a marriage bed,
filled our nostrils in each dread hour,
and now we weep,
at the harvest which we reap.
How sleep our dead, how sleep our brave,
was it for this mockery of men
their sweet lives they gave.
Or was it more than blood we spilt
to breed youth of this present ilk,
who, with throttles wide in mighty roar
down roads of peace, make sounds like war.
On sleeping villages they sweep
and leave a trail of wreckage deep
that strikes us to our very core,
these brave sons of our dead, these sons we bore.
The vandals who walk our city streets,
rip up our trains, and filled with drugs and drink
go their merry way, and make a bigger stink
than death.
Still these flowers of manhood, or should I say weeds
O'erwhelm us with their evil deeds.
Oh that these tares among our wheat
had been swiftly torn out, and only the sweet corn
allowed to grow,
to honour our men, who died so long ago.

Helen M Colthorpe-Parker

MESSAGE FROM THE DEPARTED

How silent is this garden of stone
Monuments to loved ones once here now gone
Passed through this vale of tears we call life
To a brighter world in God's loving light

Come sit by me do not be afraid
Let my spirit comfort you in your grief
Remember everything I said and did
Let me live in your heart until we meet

All earthly blessings passed away
But still I am with you each and every day
Giving you the courage to carry on
God Bless you each and every one.

Eileen Jones

YOUNG WOMAN IN AN OLD BODY

Young woman in an old body,
You were the life and soul,
Effervescent laughter,
Wicked sense of humour,
High octane liver,
Generous as a giver,
God fearing but not religious.
Ethical. 'What's ethical?' you might say
Now you are content, thank God,
Little old lady, volcano extinct,
Growing old gracefully,
Mother.

John K Wilkinson

HOME RULE FOR THE PIER HEAD

Burn all bridges flood the moat
cut the ropes and off we float
it's not long now to next high tide
and soon we're out of Merseyside

We've had enough of other folks
a long time now the butt of jokes
'cos snobs we are and snobs we stay
we'll wave tarra and drift away

Each other's trumpets we can blow
just as it was so long ago
to pass the time we'll tread the hay
as cowbells ring the *woolly way*

But oops! The world has passed us by
without a wave without a sigh
maybe they didn't know we'd gone
so just what planet are we on?

Well never mind me old sop cock
let's head on back to Albert Dock
no more the moaning minnies be
it's not so bad here near the sea

George C McIver

IN A GIRL'S HEAD ...

Sadness,
Anger,
Hate,
Wanting to lash out,
To reveal her true feelings,
Fear?

But then,
Joy,
Love,
Hope for the future,
No longer needing comfort,
Happiness,
Peace of mind.

Lauren Ketchell (13)

RICHES TO RAGS

Sitting in this strange place as faces change
From riches to rags dictates all that I know
Everything in order but somehow strange
Topless girls leer and tease but only for show
Polished shiny boots I wish were now dirty
Back on old cobble streets how they long to go
A whole new future for someone. Way past thirty?
An insane world forever will press down on me
To impose glamorous friends of course uninvited
Only the unopened Harrods bags can they see
Appointment book of champagne parties ready sighted
Family and friends have moved on to the past
The circle that once stood remains a rising wall
When everybody else has gone I sit alone at last
Look at the half empty bottle how I feel so small
The Asian Grocer neither knows who or where I'm at
That honest chatter feeding such desperate space
To enjoy a few words with sanity affirms who I am
Tissue wrapped bottle gift wrapped, smile upon face
A balanced sound punter of old, I sometimes cry
Until the voice rung out, 'It could be you,' did lie
Alone, posh people now come and smile with wares
At the successful tramp that won. Who still shares.

Michael Young

MY CHILDREN

Early in the morning
  I lie awake in bed.
I hear the children playing
  And this is what they
    said.
I'll hide by the cupboard
  And you hide in the hall,
You can be an Indian
  And make an Indian call.
I shall be a cowboy.
  And I will have a gun
When you hear bang bang
  That's when you run.
Shh, be a little quiet
  Mummy's still asleep.
Oh, no she isn't I just saw her
  peep.

Sylvia Mellon

PRECIOUS

One look from you,
Is like a summer breeze,
It makes my soul shiver.
A touch from you,
Is worth more,
More than all the precious jewels of this world.
A kiss from you is more precious than gold,
One smile from you,
Brightens a day more than the sun ever could.
To be touched by you,
To be in your arms,
Is precious.

Breige McGroggan

THE SNIP

The months of waiting are nearly over,
Now I'm tipsy, and not very sober.
I am gripped in a vice-like grip,
On a cocktail of drugs I trip.

Upon a cloud of gas and air.
I don't bother, I don't care.
Nothing is what it seems,
I have wonderful childhood dreams.

The mind slips back to another time,
As back from the ceiling I try to climb.
Through the fog I see angels in white,
What a feeling, what a sight.

Back to reality I'm calmly led,
Into my place in a hospital bed.
I gave a squeal, I gave a shout,
I thought babies just slipped out.

Come on, come on nearly there,
My baby has a head that's square.
Pushing, pushing for all I'm worth,
It's very hard work, this giving birth.

Women have babies all over the place,
I'm pushing so hard I'm blue in the face.
I look at my husband with words unsaid,
Soon *you'll* be in a hospital bed.

No more times will I make this trip,
I've booked you in to have *the snip!*

Stella Heyworth

THE FOURS

Thomas,
The 'Gangly Mantis',
Devours Warbreck's brittle attack,
Bat flashing artistically,
And with a snap of the wrists,
Caresses the ball to the boundary,
Ball blinking on its way.
Past dire fielders,
Charring hapless confidence,
And melting technique,
Flinging themselves elegantly at the red blur,
But land in a heap,
Disheartened by their fruitless effort.
The ball now retrieved,
Is once more delivered,
But crook'd elbows jutting, jab.
Skittering across the grass,
Round red fish on invisible hook,
Leaps up at the boundary rope in spasm.
Then smacks against the hoarding,
And, as in surprise at its own violence,
Springs to a stop.
Silence broken by patterned claps,
Like the snap, snap, snapping of briefcases,
And the genteel pavilion nods obligingly.

Daniel J Thomas *(13)*

THIS MOMENT IN LIFE

Old am I,
But still things I see.
This moment of life,
That was for me.

Here I stand on this lovely hill,
Waiting for my lover, still.
She is later than I thought,
Has someone else she sought?
To love her better so,
If then, from life I will go.
Without her, life ain't much worth,
But take my life, have I got the nerve?
Take it with what?
Maybe pills, a lot.
Maybe a gun,
With its barrel of fun.
Or a rope from a tree,
With my final plea.
But somehow I can't take my life,
Not even with a knife.

Here I stand on this lonely hill,
Waiting for my lover, still.
But wait, I hear a rustle,
From a bush a bustle.
It's my lover she's come at last,
So forget all I said in the past.

Old am I,
But still things I see,
Like this moment of life,
That was for me.

Neville Hicks

ESTRANGED

Estranged from the aura which surrounds
The leather-scented, scraping sounds
Of horses for the sport,
In mud, cyanic-eyed you wait,
Distraught.

Sharp splintering silence am I,
Tension-screeching inhibition,
Afraid of local strangers
From strange, local places,
Who nudge and grin in humoured recognition.
Bilious, boasting, secretive noise.

My perfected prose destroys
What must be destroyed.

B Triona Murphy

A MOMENT SHARED

Strolling through the woods today,
I came across a child at play,
The air was filled with her delight
Her small hand held a wondrous sight.

Expressions flicked across her face
Rapture in her childlike gaze.
The innocence of her pleasure,
A moment that I will treasure.

Do you want to see what I've found
It was right here on the ground.
Nestled in the tiny hand.
A ladybird she gently held.

Mary E Wigan

FAITH

My God my God
my faith I give
please take please take
so faith may live

My faith my faith
for years my light
please take please take
I have no fight

My faith my faith
I give to you
so faith my love
will make it thru

This night this night
my faith is strong
like months gone past
and days so long

My faith my faith
your pain is mine
sweet faith my love
your faith is mine

My child my child
sweet faith I must
give God your soul
in whom I trust

Sweet faith sweet faith
my child first born
my faith in God
is stronger this dawn

A Mullen

BIRD

Songbird in a gilded cage, why mock me with your song?
You sing of cheer and happiness, yet to be caged is surely wrong?
You cannot fly or choose your lot, or wander where you will;
You, like me, are locked inside with endless time to kill.

You were born to ride the winds, to soar up near the stars;
You were born to be quite free, not held behind steel bars.
I know your plight, I share it all, I feel the pain you feel;
Although I'm not inside your cage, the trap is just as real.
I know I'm here by my own hand, and I know that life's not fair,
But while I'm locked inside like this, I don't feel the warmth of care.

Locked away? That's part of it, but a part that's very small.
I could talk of shame, indignity, and hardly cover it all.
The rotten food? Shared underwear? The atmosphere of crime?
The lack of chance when you get out? It's part of doing time.

Banged to rights and locked away, my sentence really bites,
Yet though they took my freedom, I still have my human rights.

You can keep me from what's dear to me in this world of push and shove,
But none of what I've done disentitles me from love.
I'm not talking of that mushy stuff, I really wouldn't dare,
But in my life there's lots of room for simple, loving, care.

David Mears

I SURRENDERED

Surrendering everything
I allowed that kiss.
Sweet needed poison poured
Horribly on turbulent bliss.

Loathing that I loved
Bitter for something so sweet -
Had time not snatched apart
That kiss. That kiss!
I needed it, but wish
Never had it happened.
I love you and loathe you
It had to happen and it did.

Rachel Jane Holt

WIDOWHOOD

This morning I got out of bed
Where I'm glad to lay my head
I wound my way and down the stair
Into the room there was no-one there
To the kitchen make some tea
Nobody wants a cup but me
I said good morning to the wall
It didn't give any reply at all
There's not much chance someone will call
Folk all busy one and all
Recently joined the widowed band
One of the loneliest in the land
Kindly folk hand one the line
Time will pass and you'll be fine
But one knows you can't replace
A much missed and remembered face
So stand upright and must walk tall
Or into depression soon will fall
Although you feel all trouble and strife
Face it girl get on with life.

G Collinge

CANDY

She pads alongside me
Panting, a little concerned
That the path is clear ahead.
A slight change of direction,
A movement to avoid some obstruction,
Smoothly executed - unhurriedly!
Two creatures - one human
The other animal with but
One pair of eyes.
Mutual reliance transmitted
Through a short length of lead -
A leather connection between two minds
To guide the feet and body safely
Through paths so clear
To those gifted with vision.

A common sight
To the passing observer -
Yet not so. For I can see
And my dog is blind.

Bill Goodwin

SEASONAL THOUGHTS

Spring brings the crocus and daffodils too
All with their radiant beauty on view,
As they break through to a new birth
So thrilled to be born, they give a toast - to the earth.

Summer brings the roses in colourful array
With their pleasing fragrance - they are proud to be - on display;
In cottage gardens, tended with pride,
Where buzzing bees try to find - somewhere to hide.

194

Autumn brings the falling leaves
Even from the tallest of trees,
Making a carpet of russet, and gold,
As they flutter to the ground, to mould.

Winter brings the rain and snow,
Sometimes, rivers overflow,
The water gushing beyond control,
Then devastation - takes its toll.

Kathleen Knott

FRIEND

Someone beside you, in everything you do
People confide, their souls so true
Don't be a stranger, I'll be your friend
Your solemnly guide, to the very end
Believe in us, for it's we who care
Just call out our name
And we'll all be there
Take my hand, and I'll guide you through
Our village of friendship, of something new
A feeling of truth, a feeling of love
May God bless us all
From his heavens above
Laughter, fun, pain and sorrow
We will confront, bringing tomorrow
Another day, another challenge we all face
By believing in our friends, we can erase
Any dark shadows that it may cast
Believe in yourself my friend,
Because your friendship will forever last.

Nasur Iqbal

MY ESCAPE

When asked to write a poem, lyric or a rhyme
  I find it such a pleasure, and never do decline.
You see . . . I think myself a poet, of which there's very few!
  Or maybe they're just hiding from themselves, me and you!!

Our thoughts are very real to us, and panic can bring fear
  We each need ways to live our lives, my own is written here.

I love to write my feelings down, this helps me through my day
  Maybe you're as tense as me? Then try this simple way!
To write your thoughts and daydreams
  To 'dabble' where we shouldn't
This truly can be helpful if, unhappy, sad or troubled.

To climb inside your fountain pen
  Flow freely in blue ink
Relieves *all* daily tension
  And, leaves you in the 'pink'!!

Caroline S Rogan

ODE TO DUSKY

I look out to the garden, where I'd
often said, 'Nothing could give me
greater pleasure,' tend each bed . . .
Now, to joys, my heart can harden . . .
Beauty can be so, 'insignificant',
For tears I have shed . . .
Each one, to touch, a lonely, silent bed . . .
'Where, sleeps my darling' . . .
In solitude . . . like it,
And, God, you'll pardon, if I,
'Cry inwardly, instead' . . .

Kathleen A Millington

196

CHRISTMAS PAST

Christmas Eve. The bell chimes twelve and augurs Christmas Day
A handful in the church-on-the-hill gather homage for to pay.
Not thronging aisle and transept as twenty years ago
But a gathering in rear-most pews makes 'something of a show.'
The liturgy is languid now - classic phrase replaced by 'mod'
Not so much of God as the judge of men, as of 'persons' assessing God.
With amidships pandemonium that the President calls Peace
And audience participation causes ne'er a tongue to cease
Alas, alas. We've gathered there at the start of Christmas Day
Not in the Church of England, but the Church of England gone away.

Christmas Day the more perceptible, dawns clear and bright and still
The sun shines down in warmthless kind with bitter icy rill.
And the bells ring out with such clarity past river and past mill
To call good folk on Christmas morn to come to church-on-the-hill.
But they call not the traditional, to come in timelessness' sway,
Not to the Church of England, but the Church of England gone away.

Boxing Day. Church-on-the-hill stands shut - as, save a Sunday,
                                                      it always did
Its quietude reassuring now, with changefulness well hid.
In unchanged bright morn glints unchanged strong stone, unbending
                                                      and unbent.
And the unsensing soul feels permanence and firm establishment.
But the hierarchy, within the stone, has wrought another clay
Not now the Church of England, but the Church of England gone away.

N J Inkley

197

UNTITLED

You really are a clever girl,
We knew that you could do it,
You could have never looked us in the eye,
If you'd have gone and blew it,
Did you hear the bulletin
On News At Ten last night
With a warning to all motorists
To keep well out of sight,
Then when they knew you'd done it,
The all clear siren blew
And they had to call the troops out,
To hold back all the queues,
Because the streets of Wigan were crowded
With people wanting to say
How proud they were to know you
And how you'd made their day!

T Mitchinson

ENGLISH SUMMER

I'm fed up with this weather, all we get is rain,
And the howling winds make it feel so cold,
I'd love to wake some morning, to a rain free
window pane,
And feel the sunshine ere I get too old,
I cannot get my washing dry, and the gardens
are all boggy,
If I venture out down to the shops I'm bound
to come back soggy,
You take a brolly with you, the wind blows
it inside out,
So wrap up warm, put your wellies on, whenever
you go out.

Barbara Ellison

198

IMPRESSIONS OF THE 1914-18 WAR NEAR THE ANNIVERSARY OF PASSCHENDAELE 6TH NOVEMBER 1917

(Dedicated to those who lost their lives)

The curfew knell of the peace has now begun,
With cries and tears and laments,
Of the shedding of the blood to come,
And war begins with its sonorous oratory beneath,
When the guns line up in lethal symmetry asleep.

Now in booming cacophony explode the guns,
In constant repetition day and night,
Oh never was such a sight!
Here charcoal carcass trees alight,
In funeral skeletons grave might,
Declare the scene of war!

Peace there is none but a moment,
And once again the dismal dirge of sounding fire,
Strikes upon a world in winter's chill,
Where underfoot soft cracking breaks,
In melancholic thrill; the frost,
Echoing that mindless thud of death!

Ah! - Still now is the bated soldier's breath,
After gasping the acrid air
Of chlorine and of burning flesh,
Horror now has no meaning there,
For all they can do is stare!

See now what is left of Passchendaele,
But those bitter tears born of blood,
Now scarlet poppies are their yield,
And flowers flow as in a flood!

Barry Bradshaw

DEFENDING THE RING

It's not symbolic
Of a hole in the soul
That won't grow whole:
It's a hole in the nose
Where an earring goes.
So it looks like a swing
Where a budgie would sing
And flutter its wings,
But that doesn't mean the wearer's caged.
It's merely what you see,
There's nothing more to it
Than a nose,
A hole,
With an earring going through it.

Stephen Michaux

THE STORM

The storm looms threateningly above,
like a hot boil waiting to erupt,
The birds flee in fright and a cold silence, prevails,
A ferocious wind suddenly leaps over everything,
like a huge black sprawling cat.
The grass moves in waves like a green sea and the trees move as if
dancing, swaying, bending at the knee. The sky gets darker and the rain
starts, not gradually, but grossly, pelting against the window panes
and streaming down the desolate lanes.
Now lightning crackles, like wicked laughter and shows itself like
strands of silver tinsel, against the dark grey sky.
Nothing lives in this storm for it is not able.
Even the big brave dog crawls under the table.
It seems like the dead of night, although it is only three-o-clock in
the day and I pray silently, oh please storm go away.

Kathleen Tapper

THE LOST AND LONELY

The nights are long and lonely
Now that winter's coming round
The snow is falling heavily
And it's covering the ground

I wonder what the homeless do
As they have no place to go
The only covers they will have
Is blankets of frost and snow

Oh! Come on all you people
Please lend a helping hand
Give love and understanding
Help the homeless in this land

For they have nothing to look forward to
No warmth or Christmas dinner
With no family and no friends
And each day getting thinner

J M Everson

THE METRO

We ride on a tram on a railway track
With gentle sway and clickety clack,
Into the city through the street
Among the people's chattering feet,
By the cars with their smoking tails
Then back to ironways' ancient rails
A regular transport of delight
Commuting daily from morn' till night.

Marguerite Yates

THE SUMMER SUN

Where are you,
When I need you.
When the days,
Are dark and cold.
And the winter,
He has grasped me,
With his ever waiting shroud.
Where are you,
When I'm frightened.
And the nights are lasting years.
And I fill my bath,
With vinegar,
From ever flowing tears.
Where are you,
When the trees have,
Shed their leaves,
And birds do fly.
And the flowers,
Shed their sunlight,
Then bow down,
And say goodbye.
Where are you,
My dear yellow face,
The heat that never dies.
Alone behind the clouds so grey,
And cunning winter skies.
Where are you?

T F Vukasinovic

TRAVELLER

Life is a journey
We don't know where we're going,
Where it will lead,
for life uses no footways,
No highways or byways.
Life cuts its own path.
A path of roads, endless roads.
And so I journeyed on.
The months eating up the miles.
On my left, a forest of despair.
So easy, just to lose the path,
And never come out.
On my right, a chasm of broken dreams,
And broken hearts.
Still the same miles of dusty roads.
I came upon a beach,
A beach of confusion
Stretching far beyond the horizon.
And, beyond the beach, an ocean,
A sea of regret and lost time.
It made me think.
And, so I travelled home.
Just one, last mile.
And there you were.

Ruth Nixon

HEARTBREAK AND RUIN

Concrete and steel, is all we have today!
Polythene and plastic, you can't throw it away
Cement blocks and barbed wire fences
Security cameras, with zooming lenses.

Don't hold up traffic, that's on the rampage
Or someone will introduce you to, a bout of road rage
You can hear singing, from birds in the city
But they're only recordings, oh what a pity!

Don't eat any eggs? They're full of salmonella!
A woman from Spain thought they meant paella!
Don't touch any sandwiches, with beef on the bread
Or you will end up demented, and soft in the head!

Don't drink the water, it's polluted they say
Someone just tasted it, and shrivelled away!
Now don't go to the hospital, 'cos you won't get a bed
Someone went yesterday, and now they are dead!

You can't use timber, because there's no trees left
And you can't wear fur coats, 'cos all the animals are bereft!
Please don't touch anything that glows on the beach
And leave all your valuables within easy reach!

Don't swim in the sea, you may start a confusion
And alter the tide, that will change evolution!
Please don't walk in the sun, the light burns too strong
The ozones have snuffed it, where have we gone wrong?

This is my poetry, the poetry of today!
Nature has almost left us, man has chased it away!
He doesn't know what he wants, or where he is going
But all he leaves in his wake, is heartbreak and ruin!

Thomas Ian Graham

TASHA SHEBA ELIZABETH JADE

Her blackened charcoal fur
Is lit by sparks,
Burns brown and red.
Flames flicker and waltz
As suddenly the sun unlocks the grey clouds in the sky.
Her precious stones watch everything.
Smothering the world in their deepness,
Starry emerald green.
With glowing, growing reflections of the world.
Her eyes rhyme.
Translucent as images, thoughts flash through
And almost jump.
Almost I can catch sight of her words.
As the sprays of beams
Run along her body.
And slowly fade and pale-away.
Into the refreshing air
That gently blows her fur
Into ripples.
And so, as she sails on through midnight,
Day returns to darkness.
The fire is put out,
And her pool of fur
Changes into the deepness of her eyes.
No reflections,
No images.
Only when the sun shines
Can you see into her mind.

Kelly Archer (14)

DULCE AMOR INEXPERTIS

Sure as the slow graceful flow of age,
The autumn chill signals time to turn another page,
You've seen what a man can do,
I've seen the hate of a woman too.

Darkness throws its cloak towards the earth,
Our love, your life what are they worth?
Lie in the arms of sleep dreams yearning for the past,
Put them back in your locket love was never meant to last.

Once the tape starts playing we can't make it rewind,
A dream, a desire it burns in our minds,
Our hearts battle a myriad of wars,
We're losing everyone, no noble cause.

You want to leave, no more reason to stay,
You say my love has gone anyway,
Searching for the time on a clock with no hands
Perhaps love's an illusion, a mirage in the sand.
One day you may find its ephemeral domain,
Then, some say, you have won the game.

S Rumley

OUR EDITH

Eighty-one is like a dream,
To a lady born in 1914.
Edith has survived two world wars,
And owns a cat with milk-white paws.

Clad in a thin blue cotton dress,
She has no-one left now to caress.
Reconciled to existing alone,
She can't afford to chat on the phone.

Edith still recalls the good old days -
Preston fairs and Blackpool holidays.
She depends on carers to feed her now,
And manages to keep cheerful, somehow.

She never leaves her terraced house,
Frail, but contented, quiet as a mouse.
Her weak heart is gentle, loving and kind,
It's only two years since she first went blind.

Wendy Flanagan

DEATH ON A SUMMER'S DAY
(1st Battle of the Somme, 1st July, 1916)

Eighty years have come and gone
since that fateful July day,
When whistles blew
and young men died,
So many lives were thrown away.
'Over the top!' the officers cried
'Onwards to fame and glory!'
But oblivion was what they found,
Death on a summer's day.

The smoke has cleared
the barbed wire gone,
Guns that once
spat pain and blood,
Lie silent now upon the Somme,
and brave old men
with tears in their eyes
return in order to recall,
Death on a summer's day.

Carole H Sexton

THE UPPER HAND

Naiveté of nature is what all cats enjoy,
It makes it mundane madness their slyness to employ.
Cosseted on cream by day, or other such delight,
They've little inclination for catching mice at night.
Cats are cunning, coy, capricious,
Subjugate you to their wishes.
Creatures of devious deity, assuming a nonchalant air,
Queening it over the household, possessing your very own chair.
Or perched high up on the garden shed,
Surveying the neighbours sweat and toil,
Eyeing the new turned patches which by night they will despoil.
Felicitous felines of the day, menacing moggies of the night
Mesmeric monsters, they never show respite.
So I bought a dog - the dirty rat -
She just made a friend of that.

Richard Ferguson

A TALE OF A TEAR

The sun is a golden princess on her throne within the sky,
The moon, her silver husband, upon his face she often smiles,
Her tears are the many raindrops that fall from her palace above,
Whilst his grief reflects in the night sky, for each star is a tear of love.

They are separated forever by the rule of day and night,
Each alone in a separate world, together sharing light.

Long ago they bore a child, and christened her Paradise,
The greenlands were her bosom, the deep blue oceans were her eyes.
The rivers were her bloodstream, the deserts her golden skin,
Now sun and moon are grieving, for their child is wrapped in sin.

G G Jones

WILL O' THE WISP (JACK)

Jack of the lantern and Jack of the green
I'm the one you never have seen
Jack of the sea and Jack of the shore
Jack of the marsh and Jack of the moor
Jack in the box and Jack and Jill
Jack who will do no man ill
Jack can take the bitter pill
Jack who your wildest dreams can fill

Jack the soldier and Jack the tar
Jack go nowhere and Jack go far
Jack in the rushes and Jack in the tree
I can see you but you will never see me
Jack the king and Jack the knave
Jack the prisoner and Jack the slave
Jack who finds an early grave

Jack of all trades and Jack of none
Jack the father and Jack the son
Jack the foolish and Jack the bad
Jack the happy and Jack the sad
Jack the coward and Jack the brave
How could you judge someone like me
For I'm the one you never see
Even James Jacques or John?

P Goulding Snr

WHEN WE WERE YOUNG

As time goes by I think of you
And all the things we used to do
The lovely lanes we did once walk
And how we loved to talk and talk
Of all the things we would do one day
And how we'd sit and watch the children play
The sun would shine all day long
And life would be one long song.

We never dreamt that this would not be
Those days we really could not see
Our life ahead would be so much fun
And how we'd laugh and run and run
Through the meadows - buttercups ablaze
In those long ago now days and days

But now I'm old and can only dream
Of what once seems to have only been
A short time ago - but a lifetime away
Of lots and lots of yesterdays
And all our dreams have only become too
Just a memory of me and you.

Nora Billington

VAMPYR: PART 1

To the cynic, the lover and the unholy saint.
Who seems as bad as you?
Homicidal man, he puts me in irons,
I grin as I love him true.

Hearts beating overdrive, tending the innocent
Who flock to my graveside at will.
Faith heals all, all but the deep wounds
Which shed blood in the heat of the kill.

The zest of the life, sensations in flow.
Could I gorge myself until I die?
Who cares if I sit upon my immoral throne
Shedding sigh upon sigh upon sigh . . .

I left my grave early, the world now I roam.
As the blood pounds so does my soul.
A godless wonder to the loveable cynic,
And the saint?
Well, I sold him my soul.

Debra Lee

A SINNER

I gaze at your image on a metal cross,
And wonder if you're happy with this human chaos
Or are you so angry we're all damned to hell,
Because to temptation we all have fell,
We cheat and fight, lie and manipulate
Giving no thought to our eventual fate
We steal and beg not only material wealth
Like thieves we move with cunning and stealth.
Who will wipe the tears of your broken heart
As from your loving arms we depart,
Why can't we see you're our friend - our brother
The love you offer can be given by no other,
Our prayers of love have a hollow ring
So do the hymns of praise we sing,
We beg for mercy and for forgiveness
For time so our lives we can redress,
But you know us better than we know ourselves
Oh why can't I behave myself.

Pamela Steen

MESSAGES

Messages passing
over the miles
bring sometimes sadness
sometimes smiles
over the radio
or TV
a message for you
but never for me.
The postman passes my house
I fear,
perhaps he's forgotten
that I live here.
Then a message comes through
over the phone
'Hello.' 'Hello.'
'Is anyone home,'
I answer 'yes' quickly,
but who could it be
who would be sending a message
to me,
'Yes, yes,' I answer again
'I'm here,'
But mine wasn't the voice
they wanted to hear
'Sorry, wrong number,'
Someone said
then crackle-crackle
and the phone
went dead.

Kathleen Cooper

MOTORWAY JAM

Like beached whales the traffic stands,
Exhausts spouting over-pungent fumes;
Then heat-hazed bonnets gradually cool.
Inevitability reigns.
Three rows, with everywhere to go.
Wailing cars and clanging ambulance
Fly up hard shoulder.
Seat back, and take the chance to snooze,
Or hunt the wavebands for some news.

Doors slam.
Smooth salesmen socialise
With horny-handed heavy hauliers;
Tall tales are told
Of celebrated hold-ups of the past.
Across the route a car slows down
'About five miles' and wave of thumb.
Inevitability reigns.
Nowhere to go.

Then
Movement from horizon cascades closer.
Doors slam;
Atmosphere re-blighted;
Creeping, halting progress;
Columns collapse, by cones compressed.
Fluorescent coated flickering-blue faced heroes
Shift smashed shells of burnt-out dream machines
That lie stranded in glass glittering islands.
Our three-laned traffic pod re-forms.
In echelon we drive with extra care
'Til it's our turn

Roger Gibson

THE GREEN ROOM

Have you ever seen the Green Room?
A lighthouse of enigma
Enchanting momentary souls to look upward to the heaven
And wonder why?
The Green Room

No mortal nor object in the Green Room
It's calm beyond reach
Intrigued to its actuality, its motive, we fly like birds to the nest
And sedition crawls from
The Green Room

Pandora's box clutches no temptation like the Green Room
I plunge for the apple
An answer to good and bad, no stranger yet knows that hikes beneath
I wonder why
The Green Room?

Anthony Robert Stevenson

IT'S AUTUMN WHEN

It's autumn when the dying leaves
float to earth on smoke filled air,
one by one they kiss the ground
and spread their musty carpet there.

It's autumn when the spider spins
a web so fine it were of mist
when all entrapped cannot escape
but have to keep a deadly tryst.

It's autumn when the burning sun
bows down low his heavy head,
with glowing breath he brands the earth,
and outlines all a fiery red.

It's autumn when the harvest comes
the land must springtime's promise keep.
Then nature's treasures gathered in
now is the time for winter's sleep.

Carol Field

LOVE

What is love?
Is it something that comes from up above?
Is it something that harms us deep inside?
Something cold and empty, that hurts all our pride?
Or is it something that makes us feel happy?
Warm and giddy, excited and wacky,
Or is it something that fills us with sorrow?
The sorrow that we leave until tomorrow,
And then it never goes away,
And we realise that it's here to stay,
Or does it change the person we are?
For the better or the worse, maybe the better by far,
Does it make us feel like a king or a queen?
Or does it make us say things we don't really mean?
Do we ever feel the same?
As we did before the loved ones came,
Or do we feel that we have changed?
With all our feelings beginning to range,
From happy to sad,
From gloom to glad,
Or do we feel that we have lost?
Something that was precious and at our
own cost.

J Bailey (13)

ONE SPRING DAY

Purple mountains glowing,
Soft in misty dew,
The sweet smell of spring's awakening,
The world now born anew.

Springtime lambs stumble and falter,
To the warmth of Mother's side,
Finding love and nourishment,
A safe place to reside.

A field of golden daffodils,
Bright in gentle sun,
That has risen from its slumber,
Now that winter's done.

New hopes are born in springtime morns,
Old troubles washed away,
A new start, beginning, the page unsullied,
On the first new springtime day.

Caroline Wilson

DARKNESS

I feel the rain upon my face
The wind that blows around
I also feel the snowdrops
As they fall down to the ground.

Children I hear playing
Birds singing in the trees
I often do hear whistling in the breeze.

There's lots of things, I long to see
If only I weren't blind.
Maybe God will give me sight, when I pass by.
For then there will be no darkness
The Lord will give me light.
And then I'll see the beauty,
In God's heavenly paradise.

J Jones

MOTHER

Mum, she has three jobs to do
Mother, Father and Best Friend too,
Best Friend is the one she does the best
Although she does exceed in the rest.

She is feeling down and depressed at the mo'
but I want her to know that I love her so
She tells me that she has never felt so bad
and this really does make me sad

Although I don't know exactly what to say
I do think about her each and every day
Please don't feel that you are on your own
because I am here to listen to you moan!

I do try and understand exactly how you feel
but obviously I haven't been through the same ordeal
You're brave, tough and a definite fighter
Do you think I'll ever become a Writer!

Julia Hassall

BIRTHDAY

If you were to see me now what would you see.
Sun-tanned, hair done, summer clothes,
To show off, bare legs and arms.
Smiling and interested in the people around me.
Wishing me happy birthday (50 years)!

A time for taking stock, for looking back.
I wonder where I got the knack from,
To be able to change tack? Now
All that rubbish I did not need or want,
I have been able to leave behind,
To relive the things of my past that hurt,
That break your heart,
That I have misunderstood, that was great fun,
How was I to know what was to come,
I could not carry it all anymore, I let go!

In doing so I fell into a safe place,
With people who care,
Who were always there, for me to show my tears,
To show my fears.
My pain was very near, I let go!

The results are plainly evident?
Calm and confident,
My happiness cannot be dented,
I am comfortable with myself,
I have reached an age of knowing who I am,
To look ahead with hope,
To like to laugh at myself,
And not to care if I sound like a dope,
It's not that bad to be 50 years old!

I D Jones

A SIMPLE LIFE

Oh, let me work, but do not squander
  Let me build a cottage small
Where my feet do often wander
  When eventide does fall
I don't ask for riches plenty
  For it all brings trouble and strife
Give me the wide open spaces
  Give me this simple life.

Some have to live forever
  'Neath clouds of smoke and grime
Forever dodging traffic, forever
  chasing time.
They have never seen the
  beauty of nature midst the hills.

Or walked the lovely valleys
  Through which the water spills
I've faced the strongest weather
  And winds just like a knife
Still my heart is strongly
        Tethered
  Towards a simple life.

Oh, some do scheme for power
  While others who are poor
Dream of things they might have had
  If gold was 'neath their floor
And their homes great big mansions
  Set amidst the hills
Yet even then they'd worry
  How to pay their weekly bills
For me there is no worry, nor
  Want, nor fear, nor strife,
As long as there's a sun above
  Give me, my simple life.

Brian Barton

IN MY GARDEN

The butterflies, that dance around,
Upon the Buddleia I'll be bound,
Those horrid snails that take their toll
Upon all things that grow in soil.

The weeds in profusion grow,
I must arise and apply the hoe,
The roses in a distant bed
Their colours, are a lovely red,
And adjoining them in another bed
Are roses, pale yellow, pink and a paler red.

I'm afraid these roses need my attention
From the aphids, black-fly, and some cane erection.

The veg garden, looks a little glum,
That compost heap, phew, sure does hum!
This hot spell we're getting now,
Brings out all those stinging flies,
They appear to get all over even in my eyes.

A spray, I'm sure will do the trick,
But the darned smell from it sure makes me sick,
My garden gnomes, all there erect,
Around the pond I do detect,
Guarding the fish down below,
'Oh! Please excuse me. I must really go . . . '

D Gorton

A BEACON

A beacon flashes its guiding light
Into the darkness of the night
And steadfastly within a harbour it guides
Boats coming in upon treacherous tides

A beacon also saves the day
As you go upon your way
Only if you would stop and listen
To the flow of the traffic upon the road
Come seek for the green light
Then always behave as you become warned

A beacon is someone with a helping hand
So given to all in time of trouble
A beacon in faith that's what all need
To reach that hand in an hour of despair
In order to gain *consolation,* I do declare

A beacon is God's guiding light
To help us all through
Each peril of the night
E'en through a long-lost day
When so often we go astray

A beacon shows within one's eyes
As they meet a lover's gaze
E'en a child spieth a beacon
Amidst its mother's love
Oh! Safe within its beacon, *home!*

Margaret Howens

FROM TIME TO TIME

Through time and distance from when and where
Forwards backwards in circles flair.
In dreams and real paths do entwine.
In search of whims and hopes with slights
and desperates, our days are spent in what
we call our time.
If time is real and distance too when
was the start when things were new?
Is the answer in bold dreams to cast
the guides and windows to see if past is past?
Will we ever know from where, will
we ever know from when?
Will our time come round will it come again?
Is the answer found in simple faith confound sophisticate?
Is now now is then then does it
come again through our fate?

W Ward

INTRUSION

Many, many years of skimping and saving,
Gone by the board, due to vandals invading,
They enter our homes, intent on stealing,
Not bothering to consider our feelings.

Little gifts, hoarded for years,
Looking for your treasures, holding back tears,
We can never replace, things that have gone,
There were memories in each one.

The intrusion of people, entering your home,
Gives you the feeling, that you are never alone.
The havoc, the intrusion creates in your life,
Causes you to wake, in the dead of night.

The sanctuary of your home, you think is no longer there,
Your privacy invaded, what do they care,
You feel stripped bare,
This place and tranquillity, no longer there.
The peace!

M B Wild

THE OLD WIVES' TALE

We were in days long gone
  An angelic pair, inseparable
As sugar and spice.
  Amongst a giggle of school friends,
We shared girlish games,
  With fairies, goblins, dragons,
Witches and daisy-crowned queens.
  We were once a whispering pair
Of furtive teenagers,
  Sharing close-guarded secrets,
Tattling of sweethearts and scandal and promise
  As envied brides we became
Offerers of comfort and succour,
  For when the knight showed a chink in his armour,
Or rode on a mud-spattered steed.
  Even now our lives twine together,
As the dark winter's evenings enclose
  Fireside widows we sit
Seeking shelter, from the cold of the future,
  Yet basking in warmth from the past.

Clare McDonald

THE OLD DAYS

Gone are the days, that we once knew
life isn't the same anymore
neighbours were always there for each other
you'd no need to lock your front door.
When times were hard, and money was short
nobody around you would gloat
no 'Keeping up with the Joneses' then
we were all in the same old boat.
People made do with simple things
they didn't ask for the moon
unlike today, some can't pay their way
and get far too much too soon.
Children could play without any fear
at numerous games in the park
but these days, with unknown dangers about
Mum gets them in before dark.
We didn't do drugs, or molest old folks
like you see on telly these days
life was simpler then, we cared more
although we had old fashioned ways.

Mairearad Wilson

THE NON-SMOKER

They used to call it a laugh and joke
getting the fags out to have a smoke.
It seemed the natural thing to do,
a cigarette for me and you.
No cigars you understand,
just a ciggy it's a cheaper brand.
It was like a way of being polite,
I thought at first, but, not tonight.

224

It's got too much now, they are far too dear,
They are going up again tenpence I hear.
So the thing to do I think is best,
is to give the ciggies a complete rest,
and, if you still decide to smoke,
you will pay a big price and that ain't
        no joke!

Mike Graham

THE TURNING YEAR

Stuck inside a silver-plated shell
Out breaks autumn with a story to tell
Green turns to brown in front of our eyes,
As autumn and Britain make their ties.

As autumn makes its breezy plans
We the nation declare our stands
As hibernation makes its tuck
Into the tall trees we all look.

The chills always seem to bite
With shorter days and longer nights
As we walk down our dark damp streets
The heart of autumn slowly beats.

As autumn is it must decay
Sweeping summer's growth away.
The season is just one of four
With colour and change that we adore.

And so we have the golden season
When every action has a reason.

M Benson

THE FACTORY

An abscess on the horizon
A scrawled obscenity from
Which smoke spews; dense
And deadly, it hangs

Too low for steam.
Monstrous vats pile
Up side by side, metallic,
Vile and strewn across

The dead ground. The
Soil, sulpherous, barren
Is heavy with leakage
From trucks that roar

In every hour, hissing
And spilling. Nothing
Is safe. The sea,
Deceptively clear, is not

Water but poison. Air
Bleaches. And sleep
Can never quite drown
The grating scream

Of metal, nor dreams
Disguise what lurks
Beyond my curtain.

Catherine Donnelly

A LANCASHIRE PICTURE

A beauteous picture of nature born,
Across the lane a field of yellow corn,
On the awakening to a Lancashire day,
There are silver birch trees,
Alongside a flowing stream . . .
Part of life . . . not a dream.

Lanes twist broad and narrow . . .
Hedges grow tall and short,
Nesting in many is the sparrow,
At the top of yonder lane is Bracken Farm,
Dogs are barking . . . they need no alarm.

From my window on a bright sunny day,
Are a range of enchanting hills seen,
Along with the edge of a lovely forest,
Borders are they of the Lake District,
Making a beauteous picture and scene.

There are unique villages dotted here and there,
Some are white, some are pink and blue, cottages,
Their finishing style is a roof of thatch,
Their quaintness is hard to match,
All have a market on different days,
Where people pick up bargains in lots of ways.

Lancashire hast been known for industrial times,
Cotton mills, coalmines and much more,
Granted not all things last,
Yet Lancashire holds a magic . . .
And dark secrets of the past.

Anita M Slattery

THE VILLAGE FAIR

The trestles are set all the people are there
Jostling around at the village fair
There are bottles of this and jars of that
And a stall where I saw my old Sunday hat
There's a coconut shy and a hoop-la stall
And cans to knock down with a wooden ball
There's a treasure hunt in a bed of sand
And a queue already at the sweetie stand.
Trying to name the big rag dolly
Could it be Sandra, Joan or Polly?
Who wants a go in the Lucky Dip?
Watch the children come with a hop and a skip.
Look at the apples, carrots or cauli
I love the flowers piled high on the trolley.
Races to run and games to play
I'm glad we prayed for a lovely day!
Little Rebecca in a hat of plain straw
Looks very sweet if a trifle demure.
She's wearing a dress of pale blue - with a sash on
But drags her balloon in precarious fashion,
Is that the lady who opened the fair?
She's wearing a hat you and I wouldn't dare!
Do you want some tea or a cool lemonade? -
Oh I really must watch the kiddies parade!
I say! Can you think of a nicer way
To spend a lovely summer's day?

Marjorie Densley

UNTITLED

I wonder if it's natural
To be constantly confused
I wonder if it's healthy
To be so easily amused
I wonder if it's wise to feel
That most things aren't exactly real
And cry when people order veal
And never get refused

I wonder if it's wrong to lie
Without a damn good reason
I wonder if it's bad of me
To hate the summer season
I wonder if it is a sin
To often need to make a din
To stop the ghosts from creeping in
Can selfishness be treason

I wonder if it's nice to be
Reliable and steady
I wonder if all adults
Feel the need to hug a teddy
I wonder if I'll ever know
Just when I should reap or sow
And when it's time for me to go
I doubt if I'll be ready

Sally Carruthers

THE WONDERFUL WORLD OF THE SURGEON

I watched one night on our TV,
What was very interesting to see.
Surgeons who met from countries afar,
To discuss new operations on open heart.
It is marvellous what can be done today,
The way the excess muscle was taken away.
Unfortunately for some patients it was not meant to be,
This new break-through, they have to experiment to see.
These clever clever people who choose this occupation,
Thank God there's people with so much determination.
Much skill is needed for Open Heart,
Plus many funds to do their part.
So long live our surgeons, the experts with the knife,
Who aim to bring us quantity and above all quality . . .
In our lives.

Janet Elizabeth Isherwood

THE SCARECROW MASSACRE

Can you see the shadows
In the street
Dancing all around us
On silent deadly feet?

They come for us at night
They know we cannot fight
The masks of black
And shotgun blasts
The rat-a-tat of
Planned attack

The hunt will run
Till day
Then the shadows slip
Silently away

The sun will find us
Peace of mind from
The horror of the dark
And then they found
The *alleyway*, where
Two street scarecrows lay.

J A Brewer

LIFE AMONGST THE COMMON PEOPLE!

Living here as I do, I want to tell you it's of little worth
Drug addiction everywhere needles lying here and there.
As you walk you'd better be aware,
muggings, gang rapes, attacks of all kinds.
Just you make sure you keep it in mind.
Numerous pregnancies, life on the dole,
not enough money for even coal.
Evenings in the pub *meals* at the chippy
hanging around looking like a hippy.
No goals in life nowhere to go,
watching on the box waiting for a show.
Illiteracy everywhere, barely capable of speech
even an Access course seems well beyond reach.
How I wish to move and be out of Farnworth's leechy reach,
and escape the Clampet neighbours with their drunkenness for keeps.

Mercedes Jordan

MECHANICAL WEEDS

Overnight they seem to grow like the awesome garden weeds,
Red and black, blue and green, every colour meant to be seen.
They smoke and puff, grind and groan, rattle shake and squeal,
Rushing here and rushing there stopping only for a meal.
A great long tube from a tall thin tank provides their food and drink,
Then off they go at breakneck speed as quick as the eye can blink.
Hospitals are here and there to mend their damaged bodies,
Some do not survive but live again as a new-born carbon copy.
Special roads and tracks are made for them to ride at pleasure,
Like Catherine wheels they go round and round at
speed or at their leisure
Some get stolen, some get scratched, some are loved and cherished,
Others end up in a heap amongst the ones that perished,
Each one has a family name and a special number in a book,
What a pity they can't be made to wash and clean and cook.
Life and limb are now in danger from these fierce things,
Must the sidewalks have a barrier or should we all grow wings?
Oh! Mr Ford what did you do when you invented the motor car,
They spread like measles everywhere leaving a permanent scar.

Eve Clucas

GRADE 1 LIFESAVER'S AWARD

A woman smiled
at me
today
on the
street.

She was beautiful.
She must have been
a saint.

I went home and
thought about
her,
and the
razor blades
stayed
on the shelf.

Trevor Mitchell

PENNINE STONE

Oh, what tales you could tell
As you stand all alone
On the side of the lonely moor
Where only the winds do moan
Crumbling, falling, decaying
The walls that were built to last
Left to the elements of time
And echoes of the past.
The life they held within
Has gone with the hours of time
To try and find a better life
Only sheep in the ruins climb
But all might not be lost
For who knows maybe one day
Someone might come and renovate
You to your fine old way.

Keith Towers

CITYSIDE COUNTRY

The sun begins to set over an empty horizon -
Releasing its final warmth to the cold green land.
Screams of joy can be heard echoing from the concrete village
Which no noise pollutes from the natural world.

The birds will sing in the morning
(If you are lucky)
They'll sing a song of what there is . . . nothing more . . .
And it'll be heard by the populace
Blaring from their radios
As they don't recognise their own voices . . .

But, hey, come on!
It'll be worth it
Just think of seeing a million outsiders' smiling faces
As they rejoice in the sweetness
Of turning another nothingness into good . . .
Let them throw their money at us
And we'll just do what we always do . . .
No money can turn this into something better than it already is!
But without the artificial it will mean nothing to so many
And only everything to Society's worthless man.

The birds never really stop singing . . .
We just stop listening . . .
You can't expect me to believe that a mobile phone is more tuneful
Or a computer more imaginative . . .?

Or am I just stupid enough to have stayed in the past
Without telling the world that I left for a future a long, long time ago . . .?

Rebecca Bennett

OWING IT ALL TO HELEN

This night is alive
Suffocating green and navy sky
Stars without souls
Just rocks that exist
I'm low on self-esteem
Desperate for respect and purpose
I'm looking stressed out
I need to speak my mind
Offending and hurting those I love
I hope that they realise
That I don't mean it
Mood swings out of control
Pulling the devil by the tail
Easy to figure it out
Read between the lines
No escape from dark thoughts
They follow everywhere I go
In the shower, in my bed
I'm losing sleep again
Going to Buenos Ayres
But I do it just for fun
Eyes are a nightmare
They see right through
No sign of love they give
Nor farewell or recognition
I stole the lines
Made them mine
Waiting for the morning
Patience hurts a weary mind
Pray for time to shine.

David O'Connor

TWIRLYS

When you want to put your feet up
You no longer have to fret,
Because the day that you retire
You join the Twirly set.

You've earned the right to stand and queue
Outside the post office door,
And talk with all your Twirly friends
Of days that went before.

Why do you call us Twirlys?
I hear you all exclaim!
Well let me tell why that is
And how you got that name.

You know you get a bus pass,
But not so long ago,
That pass was used at off-peak times,
They've changed it now you know.

So at the stop you'd arrive
Before your pass was due,
Then ask *'Am I too early?'*
That makes you Twirly thro 'n' thro.

A pensioner you are not
It's plain for all to see,
You're definitely a Twirly
I'm sure that you'll agree.

If you still don't understand
Think of how it's said,
You replace the 'I' with an 'A'
If you're Liverpool born and bred.

Now put it all together
And say it really fast,
'Am-a-too-early,' that's the way
You've got it! Great! At last.

Patricia Kirk

THE VISITOR

Green hills gently rolling outward,
Downward slope to meet green field,
Birds flying to and fro from hedgerows
Clearly glad that spring is here.
But for now, tired city eyes are happy just to gaze
On gentle green hills, bathed in early spring haze.
The daffodils golden, fresh and pretty,
A welcome sight to the visitor from the city.
He wonders how long before man and his fumes
                                        will invade,
Even this serene and tranquil glade.
It seems so senseless, wrong and a pity,
Muses the visitor from the city,
That man in his pursuit for perfect environment
                                        and peace,
By his very actions, the chance of obtaining this he
                                        does decrease.
So for an ever shortening time, the visitor drinks
                                        in the view,
To store in his memory, for some future time, and rue.
And sadly the visitor realises that soon,
All too damn soon,
That this scene, so green and pretty,
Will only be seen, in pictures, in a gallery, in a city.

Eileen Buckley

THE CIRCLE
(In memory of Stuart L Summers)

A circle of friends
An invisible bond
Joined with our love
Joined in our sorrow

United we stand
Together always
One friend in the centre
He always will stay

Stuart who left us
One Sunday in May
In paradise now
On earth we must stay

A circle of friends
Around him we stand
Our hearts are all with him
We hold each other's hand

The tears sometimes fall
We kiss them away
The laughter will follow
We remember those days

You live in our souls
This circle so tight
You live in our hearts
Your flame burns so bright

Elsa M Summers

SWINGS AND ROUNDABOUTS

On the mat the gas bill falls,
Soon after, the mortgage calls,
The need for money, reality sets in,
I'll have to approach my next of kin.

Visiting the Jobcentre becomes a chore,
I hate that feeling when I go through that door,
My brain feels unstimulated, I feel such a bore,
Even my attire looks now so poor.

I know the jobs soon off by heart,
There's not much change so then I depart,
Tomorrow is another day,
One step nearer for my pay.

Below the breadline standards drop quick,
Visits to the doctor, I'm regularly sick,
The benefit I receive is not enough,
The Government I feel, don't know their stuff,
Why do people turn to crime?
Got no money and too much time.

What's a person supposed to do,
When identity goes and you're no longer you,
Self-esteem and pride drop low,
As you no longer feel and have that glow.

I need to think straight, get back on track,
I don't want to end up a statistic on crack,
How do Government expect you to live,
You're trapped in the system, you've nothing to give.

So what I'm saying in a roundabout way,
Is that your life will swing and sway,
But please remember at the end of the day,
That patience and persistence will really pay.

K A Robertson

WHY?

Why keep trying to absorb it?
When for what you can foretell
is that you may not see tomorrow;
all things have not been well!

Why think you might record it
when so oft that seems quite fruitless;
no point to pray or expect to stay.
Oh sorrow.

Why seek recall? Those nights of lights
and days of noise and thunder.
Listen, and wince to fear the shrapnel
pattering down to still us.

Why, eyes forced to open, hair on end,
whilst waspish Spandaus titter;
tottering in the slit-trench litter.
Gambling with anti-soldier mines
sown there just to kill us.

Why brave-out the stink and cold and dark;
so many rent asunder, or strive to live
and even, give; survive among the hungers.
'Gainst heat and thirst, the wounds
and dirt. Just curse, those sights
and wrongs versus the rights.

But when the guns of hatred are made silent
then we could all achieve true peace and calm,
and at last inherit God's free bounty, safe,
full saved from this life's evil harms.

Arthur Rowell

WHISKERS

My late lamented grandad oft commented
On the vast amount of precious time expended
O'er the mundane, matutinal task of shaving,
Unsightly and obtrusive stubble erasing.

Now (my grandfather being a sage old bird),
When my impressionable ears such wisdom heard,
I applied my brain to certain calculations,
Wishing to verify his observations.

I imagined a callow youth of sixteen year
In the bathroom, grinning, with his shaving-gear:
Brush, razor, foam, on this the first occasion
Of the vital ritual, the whisker-operation.

I hypothesised that, thenceforth he did have
Ten minutes every day on his wet shave
Until, at the age of six and eighty years,
He left for a happier land this Vale of Tears.

On removing whiskers he'd thus spent seven decades,
Plus many hard-earned pennies on razor blades;
And the minutes at the mirror that he'd spent
Each morn, all added up, are equivalent

To starting shaving on New Year's Day,
When strains of Auld Lang Syne have faded away,
And carrying on, with no moment's respite,
Till June, when meadows laugh in summer light.

Our life is short (just three score years and ten
Says the Good Book); yet, it would seem, some men
Spend six months of their span on merely shaving -
Surely a sobering thought worth contemplating.

Ian Whalley

A TRAVELLER'S TALE

We meet all kinds of people when travelling abroad,
We've met a judge from Surrey, and once we met a Lord,
We've met a London fireman and the captain of a schooner,
But the craziest pair we ever met were girls named Anne and Una.

They come from good old Ireland, which explains a lot of things
Anne's the one who laughs a lot and Una always sings.
We met them every morning, sunbathing on the roof,
We didn't know how daft they were but soon we got the proof,
They said they'd been there seven times and said it wasn't bad,
And anyone who thinks like that must be bloody mad.

If you travel overseas look out for Anne and Una,
You'll see them eating chips and egg and wish you'd met them sooner,
The girls are easily recognised, you'll know them when you see them,
You'll see them walking down the street, with just 3 shoes between them.

Cliff Fairclough

INFORMATION

We hope you have enjoyed reading this book - and that you will continue to enjoy it in the coming years.

If you like reading and writing poetry drop us a line, or give us a call, and we'll send you a free information pack.

Write to

Poetry Now Information
1-2 Wainman Road
Woodston
Peterborough
PE2 7BU